The Ph.D. Survival Guide

The Ph.D. Survival Guide

Eric Jay Dolin, Ph.D.
Illustrated by Dave Carpenter

iUniverse, Inc.
New York Lincoln Shanghai

The Ph.D. Survival Guide

iUniverse books may be ordered through booksellers or by contacting:

iUniverse
2021 Pine Lake Road, Suite 100
Lincoln, NE 68512
www.iuniverse.com
1-800-Authors (1-800-288-4677)

ISBN-13: 978-0-595-35030-8
ISBN-10: 0-595-35030-5

Printed in the United States of America

Contents

Acknowledgments

I couldn't have written this book if I hadn't lived through the Ph.D. process. In 1995, after 6 1/2 years in the Department of Urban Studies and Planning at the Massachusetts Institute of Technology (MIT), I became Dr. Dolin. For that I want to thank my Ph.D. Committee, which helped me make it to the end in one piece. To protect my committee members' reputations and give them the option of denying any involvement with me or my Ph.D., I will not name them here. But they know who they are, and I want to thank them for being so supportive and not laughing at me while I was in their presence.

My parents were always there when I needed them during my doctoral program, in good times and bad, with one exception. But worry not folks. I don't hold it against you for moving to another state during my sixth year in the program without telling me. That was a tough year and I understand that you just needed to get away—from me, your only son, who cried for weeks and weeks until I found you with the help of *America's Most Wanted*. I harbor no grudge, but I still can't tell you when you'll see your grandchildren, who are now 5 and 7.

To my sister, your pep talks and advice were invaluable. I especially remember the time you told me to take a magic marker and write the words "stop sniveling" on my bathroom mirror. I did it on what just happened to be the day that a close friend of mine showed up unannounced. I tried to erase the words from the mirror, but I couldn't get them off before he had to use the bathroom. When he came out, he was laughing. From then on, whenever he saw me on campus he would say, "so, have you stopped sniveling yet?" Thanks sis.

And to my wife, Jennifer, what can I say except thank you and I love you. If I hadn't met you those many years ago, I am sure I never would have gotten my Ph.D. When I was down and depressed, you were there. When I was immature and whiney, you were there. When I needed a kind word you were there. But, most importantly you were there when I needed money to pay for things like lunch and books, especially during the last year and a half of my doctoral program when I was essentially a kept man. I often reflect wistfully on that time. And always, the same question comes to mind; namely, do you think we can ever recapture the financial relationship we had back then? If we could, I promise that this time I will do the dishes and the laundry at least once a week.

If just one person buys this book and laughs and gains some insights into the Ph.D. process, then I will be happy. But I would be much happier if 30,000 people buy the book, whether they like it or not, because with sales like that I would finally be able to pay off my graduate school loans!

1

Introduction

The Ph.D. process is intense and serious, but there is also a humorous way of looking at it. This book shows you the funny side of getting what is affectionately referred to as a "Fud," while at the same time offering practical advice for surviving the process. Topics include picking a school based on its location, pleading for acceptance, identifying subspecies of *Homo doctoratus*, avoiding professorial deadwood, selecting courses that won't kill you, qualifying for a platinum copying card, raising jargon to an art form, interacting with friends and family members who think you're pathetic, footnoting your way to nirvana, sucking up to your professor's secretary, picking yourself up off the floor after the dissertation defense, and reentering the real world.

This book is intended for four audiences: Ph.D.s, those that are thinking of entering a doctoral program, those who are in the process of completing a doctorate, and those who know someone who is getting a degree. Anointed doctors should read it to relive the years or decades they spent toiling in the hallowed halls and ivory towers of academia, remembering all the while that no matter how they feel about the process, it's over, and laughing about the past is better than crying. For prospective students, please keep in mind that satire is built upon varying degrees of truth. Therefore, the more you laugh at the situations described in this book the more carefully you should weigh the decision to go to graduate school. For those who have already taken the plunge, please use this book as a diversion from your studies. All work and no play may help you get tenure one day, but it's no way to live. Finally, if you are familiar with the Ph.D. process only because you know someone getting a Ph.D., you should read this book to be enlightened. Before deciding to injure your friend, lover, spouse, or more distant relative on account of their behavior during the Ph.D. process, you must understand what they're going through. That knowledge may make you more compassionate or confirm what you already suspect; namely, that any person that pursues a Ph.D. needs professional help.

There are many interpretations of what Ph.D. stands for, including the following: Patiently hoping for Degree; Professorship? hah! Dream-on; Please hire, Desperate; Pathetic hopeless Dweeb; Probably heavily in Debt; and Particularly hapless Dude. Perhaps the best way to understand what a Ph.D. is all about is to remember what a wise person once said: B.S. stands for Bull Shit, M.S. for More of the Same, and Ph.D. for Piled hire and Deeper. Prepare to find out just how deep it can get.

2

To Be or Not To Be a Ph.D.

The first step on the way to becoming a doctoral student is deciding that you want a Ph.D. This is not an easy decision. You must carefully consider your reasons for wanting the degree and make sure that those reasons are sound. Given how long and hard doctoral programs can be, it is important that you choose your course wisely. The following is a list of bad and good reasons for pursuing a Ph.D.

Bad Reasons

Nothing Better to Do. This is probably the worst of all possible reasons. Getting a doctorate requires dedication, determination, hard work, perspiration, and inspiration. If you have no compelling reasons to pursue a doctorate, you will not exhibit any of these characteristics, and will therefore never graduate. You will also quickly discover that there are in fact many better things to do, or at least many more enjoyable ways to waste time and avoid making life decisions.

I Don't Want to Work. Are you nuts! As noted above, getting a doctorate is hard work, really hard work. If you try to coast, you'll soon have to drop out. People who claim that being a student isn't hard work are like those who claim that being a stay-at-home-parent is easy. They don't know what they are talking about.

Find a mate. Don't bet on it. Overworked, poor, and tired doctoral students who spend more time at the library than they do in their apartment are not exactly ideal "marriage material." They need time to ripen and mature, just like a good melon.

Good Reasons

Love of Learning. A good doctoral program is a feast for the brain. Almost every day you will encounter something new and exciting that will expand your understanding and appreciation for the course of study that you have chosen. If learning and exercising your mental faculties is what you love, then there is likely no better place to be than in a good doctoral program.

A Consuming Passion. If your general love of learning is complimented by a consuming passion to know as much or more than anyone else about a particular subject, that is another good reason to consider a doctorate. While the main goal of college is often to impart a liberal education, the main goal of graduate school is to give you a very specialized education. This is especially true for Ph.D. programs, where, each year on your way to graduating your focus will become narrower and narrower, culminating in an in-depth and very specific dissertation. If you pick your dissertation topic well, you will be able to sate your passion while getting your degree.

The Desire to Teach and Do Research at the Post-Secondary Level. To become a tenured professor you usually need to have a Ph.D. in your field. Although there are exceptions to this, they tend to prove the rule. A Ph.D. is both a rite of passage and a requisite credential for initiation into the professorial ranks. If you love research and want to teach at a college or university and have the security that tenure affords, then those are good reasons for getting a doctorate, for you will have the greatest chance of attaining your goals with that degree.

And now, the little known top five reasons why people pursue Ph.D.s:

5. Temporary insanity

4. Took a wrong turn on the way to the grocery store

3. Forgot to leave the university after completing a masters degree

2.   Always wanted to have business cards with Ph.D. after your name

1.   Like to play doctor.

3

Picking the Right School

You are entering into the most grueling and debt-producing stage of your life and want to make the right choice about which Ph.D. program to attend. The school you choose will determine to a large extent what you learn, the quality of the teaching, the types of people and experiences that will mold your world view, your social life, the contacts you will make, the jobs you will pursue right out of school, and how people will react to your educational background. Don't get uptight. The school you attend does not cement your destiny. Success is up to you no matter where you go. Graduates of all types of schools get good jobs and have fulfilling lives, both because of and despite their educational pedigree. Still, don't discount the critical nature of this choice. It's an important decision, and before making it you should talk to everyone whose opinion you value.

Just don't become as neurotic as the Ph.D. students I partied with one night during my first year as a doctoral student. A few of them were married with toddlers. The conversation was going great until we broached the topic of nursery school. The parents discussed the pros and cons of various schools in the area and the difficulties of getting accepted. The gist of the conversation was that unless your kid gets into the best nursery school, their chances of going to the best elementary school, high school, and college would be jeopardized. One woman even said that so-and-so nursery school was a "pipeline to Harvard." And that wasn't the worst of it. These little kids, or I should say, their parents, had to prepare in-depth nursery school applications that included recommendations. What, I wondered, could you write in a recommendation for a three-year old??!! He plays well and is potty-trained? No, the

7

recommendations for the kids of these fast-track parents probably read more like, "he has mastered finger paints, reading picture books, programming the VCR, and he is a shoe-in for a Nobel Prize in 30 years." I'd hate to be around when these kids prepare to head off to college, let alone graduate school.

Don't go to extremes. There is rarely a "right" and "wrong" when it comes to graduate schools. There is, however, better and worse. So choose wisely. As any Ph.D. would tell you, your choice should be based on a theory of decision-making, and there are many theories to choose from. You will most likely select a combination of theoretical justifications that best reflects your prejudices, hopes, and desires.

Academic Theory

According to this theory your choice is based on the quality of the teaching and the school's reputation. Ideally, these two elements are correlated, and the schools with the best and most inspiring professors are the ones that enjoy the best reputations within the academic community. Unfortunately, such a link doesn't always exist.

Academic reputations, especially at top-tier schools, are often based largely on the quality and quantity of publications one produces, along with the grant dollars one can bring into the institution. Teaching merit usually takes a back seat in both tenure positions and how one is perceived by other academics. Thus, at some universities you can end up with famous professors who are so busy outside of class that they devote little time and effort to teaching and mentoring the next generation of scholars. In a system set up like this, it should come as no surprise that doctoral students often complain about poor teaching and a lack of time with professors. Conversely, you can go to a school where the teaching is wonderful, but your main professors haven't published anything significant for years or even decades. Here the lectures may soar and the professors can spend hours discussing ideas, but they may be minor figures in the field who are less able than their counterparts at other schools to get grants and open doors for you after graduation. There are, however, many graduate schools that combine the best of both worlds—excellent teaching and impressive scholarship. Make sure that the schools you are considering fall into this category.

Location Theory

Here the choice of schools is based on three things—location, location, and location. After a long day in the library, looking up references in arcane journals where the selection criteria for articles appears to be directly related to the length of the sentences and number of five-syllable words, you've got to ask yourself what do you do to relax and have fun? Since the answer is constrained by the cultural and physical environment at your doorstep, you must take location into account. There is a big difference, for example, between going to a small, rural college where cow-tipping is all the rage, and going to school in a big city where you can eat your way around the globe without ever leaving the area.

Location also determines the population you encounter and the friends you make, platonic and otherwise. This is especially important if you are intent on meeting the mate of your dreams or just getting a date for the weekend. While it may only take one person to make you happy, it is undoubtedly easier to meet that person if there is a good size pool of people from which to choose. If you're the picky type, the bigger the pool the better. And, if you're a really neurotic, picky type who complains about almost everything, don't worry about meeting anybody, because who would want to spend time with you anyway? Also, if you have some very particular constraints with respect to dating, you best make sure those constraints can be met. For example, if you're a single, orthodox Jew from New York, who is looking for an orthodox Jewish wife, Notre Dame may not be the best place to go. But, you never know. God works in mysterious ways!

As for the married or seriously attached student, you must consider your significant other's well being. What will she do while you're at the library all hours of the night? Where will he go? Having already made a sacrifice to move to a new area, your partner won't want a life that revolves entirely around you and your academic program. You may find your work engrossing, but your partner will likely not vicariously experience the same thrill that you get from devising research methodologies or testing hypotheses. Nor will your partner want to hear incessant complaining about how demanding your main professor is or how difficult it is to come up with an original research question.

Without something else to excite your partner's mind, something else for him or her to do, your nightly discussions about school will increasingly fall on less interested ears. The half-life for the patience of those living with Ph.D. students is extremely low. Sometimes it takes only a few weeks before the significant other loses all semblance of humanity, either turning into a quivering mass of jelly or beating the doctoral student in question to a pulp. In some cases, to keep from being sucked into the sewer of despair and desperation that often opens under the feet of doctoral students, the significant other will ignore the cries for help, rationalizing that reaction with the simple refrain, "you're the one who wanted a doctorate, not me." Unfortunately, many relationships do not survive the stresses and strains of the Ph.D. experience. You can help avoid contributing to this phenomenon by keeping in mind location, location, location.

Leisure Theory

If academics alone are too narrow a pursuit for you, consider the amenities that the school offers. When you're not in class what is there to do on campus? Evaluate the athletic facilities. Is the weight room a 15' by 15' cube, with a rusting weight machine, a few mismatched dumbbells, and a sickly, yellow light coming from the fixture overhead? Are posters of the basic food groups on the wall? Does the basketball court have potholes and is the locker room the ideal place to conduct a science experiment on fungal procreation? What about the campus hangouts? Is the school pub a depressing, lifeless pit where the beer is flat and the popcorn stale? As for intramural activities, does the sailing club meet in the pool?

None of this will do if productive leisure is your goal. You want gargantuan athletic facilities that house weight rooms with twenty rowing machines, thirty stationary bikes, hundreds of dumbbells and free weights. The locker rooms must be luxurious, with a towel service, sauna, steam bath, and masseuses on demand. Shaquille O'neal should be honored to play on the school's basketball courts and the intramural program should have its own impressive facilities, including a 2,000-seat amphitheater for fencing. The school shouldn't only have a pub, but an entertainment complex where you can pick from 8 first-run movies and dine on Mexican, Italian, Chinese, or French cuisine. Doctoral programs are too long to focus solely on academics. Live it up.

Job Theory

You may tell all your friends and family that the main reason you're getting a Ph.D. is because it satisfies your love of learning. That may well be true, but that shouldn't be all. You may want to learn, but you also want to get a job. Ph.D.s, like other people, enjoy the finer things in life, like a regular paycheck, and to get those means that you'll have to work for a living. Unless, of course, you have a trust fund or have recently won the lottery. To those people, I would simply ask why do you want to get a Ph.D. when you have all that money? With a few well-placed donations to your favorite college you could probably buy yourself an honorary doctorate or at least get a building named after you.

To apply this theory to a school you must ask whether recent graduates are employed. If the school doesn't have that information or won't divulge it, you don't need to be a Ph.D. to know you don't want to go there. If such information is available, examine it very carefully and make sure you understand what it says. For example, if it is an engineering program you want to enter, be wary of programs where most recent graduates list "sanitary engineer" or "fuel-injection specialist" as their line of work. Not that there is anything wrong with being a garbage man or a gas station attendant, but, as of right now, a Ph.D. in engineering is not a pre-requisite for such jobs. In fifty years, things may be different. Or, if you're interested in business management think twice about a doctoral program that pumps out "coordinators of external telecommunications." Answering phones is an important occupation, but is learning how to do it proficiently worth six years of study?

4

The Visit

Seeing is believing, and before you pick a school you should visit the campus and "kick the professors" so to speak (when you graduate you may also want to kick the professors, though for different reasons). Try to visit as many of your prospective professors as you can. When you walk into a professor's office, you will notice a number of things, that is, as long as you're not so nervous that you can't see straight. Every professor has shelves full of books. Your initial thought will probably be that the professor has read them all and he must be really smart. That is probably true, but be more discerning before jumping to conclusions. Look carefully at the books and keep in mind the following rules of thumb. If most of the books look old and are covered with dust, you may be in the company of one of the most dangerous kinds of professors—the ossified academic. The books are probably ones the professor bought when he was a student. It is possible that his thought processes and perspectives are still rooted in the "good old days" and that none of the more recent scholarship can quite compete with what he learned at school. To make sure, quiz him on current events. Ask what he thinks of the recent books you've read. If his eyes glaze over or he starts sentences with "when I was in graduate school," beware. Working under him will keep you seriously out of touch.

If most of the books are ones that the professor wrote, and if reprints of her articles are laid out nicely on a table near where you're sitting, you are face-to-face with a person whose ego might appear large, but is, in fact, most likely quite small—the insecure academic. Stay away from this person. Be especially worried if such a professor offers to sell you one of her books and autograph it on the spot.

Another thing to keep in mind during your visit is time and attention. Does the professor keep you waiting for your appointment to begin? Is the secretary too scared to knock on his door to let him know you're there? Do graduate students straggle in, begging the secretary for time, any time, with the professor? Does the secretary respond by penciling students in for an appointment two months hence? When you're in the room, is the phone ringing off the hook and does the professor instinctively reach for the receiver? If the professor seems stretched to the limit and more responsive to the phone than you, be forewarned. There is no reason to assume that things would be better if you were one of his students.

During your meetings with prospective "mentors," listen carefully to what they say. Many statements contain hidden meanings or might not be completely accurate. Consider the following statements and potential alternative interpretations.

Someone with your excellent background should be able to get your Ph.D. in four years.

Hidden meaning: I've seen hundreds like you, who are smart, energetic, and ready to conquer academia in short order. If you're independently wealthy or are willing to take out huge loans and can focus entirely on classes and the dissertation every day, you have a pretty good shot at finishing within four years. If, on the other hand, you can't afford to rack up huge debts and you have to work to make ends meet, then you better plan on six years at a minimum; seven or eight is not unusual.

I give all my students plenty of guidance. It's my job to be a mentor.

Hidden meaning: I'm really busy. You'll be lucky to get a half-hour of my time a week, that is, of course, when I'm on campus. As my notoriety within the field expands, I will have to spend more time at meetings and getting published. I've got my career to think of. As for mentoring, consider yourself lucky if you turn out like me.

If you write a good dissertation, there will be an academic job waiting for you.

Hidden meaning: The competition is fierce out there. Colleges and universities are downsizing, but graduate schools like us keep pumping out doctorates. Don't worry though, there are other places besides academia that hire people with Ph.D.s. If all else fails, get used to saying the following: "you want fries with that?" And, hey, at least the unemployment counselor will call you "Doctor."

You should take a wide variety of courses so you have a good working knowledge of the field. You can specialize during the dissertation.

Hidden meaning: Your success will depend on your ability to know more than anyone else about a particular subject. Given the number of people in the field, that inevitably means specializing in ever more obscure topics. The sooner you become an expert in some small area, the better positioned you will be to shine and have your research published in obscure journals that are read by the other 50 people who have interests similar to yours. Remember, you're not here to become a renaissance man, but to become employed. If you're lucky, you'll attend conferences in exotic places where all the other participants are as specialized as you. If you get bored, there's always plenty of sightseeing to do. Why do you think they always have conferences in exciting resort areas anyway?

We'll get you some office space.

Hidden meaning: Down the hall is a small, windowless room, with poor ventilation, constantly humming, incandescent lights, and uncomfortable furniture. That is where you will spend your days and nights.

Being a teaching assistant (TA) is the best way to see if you can teach and to learn what it takes to be a professor.

Hidden meaning: Your main task as TA will be to respond to students who are upset that I don't spend enough time with them. You will also grade many, if not all of the class tests and papers. You will have to stall the class when I'm running late, and on rare occasions you will have to prepare a class lecture on short notice and present it in my absence. All of this valuable experience will make it clear that being a professor is much better than being a TA.

I keep in touch with most of my graduate students and they are all doing great things.

Hidden meaning: Once a student graduates, he's on his own. I hear from a few of them but rarely respond. I'm just too busy with my new students who, incidentally, are still under my control and are involved in projects that benefit me. Occasionally, I knock into past students at conferences and meetings. If they don't see me, I duck into the nearest bathroom to escape detection. If I'm caught, I feign ignorance of the year they graduated and the topic of their dissertation. And if that fails, I tell them all about my latest research and the high quality of my current graduate students. Most of my graduates go on to do great things, but since I hear from so few of them, I really can't be more specific.

The labs are stocked with state-of-the-art equipment.

Hidden meaning: We are firmly committed to the theory, "if it isn't broke, don't fix it," and the corollary theory, "if it doesn't work, theorize results." Our last operating budget for the lab was $2 million dollars. Unfortunately, that was ten years ago when it opened. Since then, the lab budget has been zeroed out to make additional funds available for football. On the positive side, we are great at repeating old experiments that are, after all, the foundation for all groundbreaking work, which, unfortunately, you can only dream about. We will be able to visit a few modern labs during your stay, and if I can create enough of a diversion, we just might get some new equipment.

The administrative staff is very helpful and will make your stay as pleasant as possible.

Hidden meaning: In the departmental hierarchy, doctoral students rank dead last. Above you are, in descending order, God, the University President, the department chair, all the professors, undergraduates, master's students, alumni, prospective students, and janitors, and the people wandering the halls looking for directions. There is, however, one staff person who places doctoral students on a pedestal—Betty. She is a fixture in the department. Unfortunately, for you, she is a very old and slightly senile fixture. She will try to help you out if she can remember your name and why you are in her office.

We have a very high professor to student ratio.

Hidden meaning: If you count all of the regular, adjunct, affiliated, visiting, and emeritus professors in the department, we have a ratio of 1 to 10. If you add in deceased professors, the ratio is 1 to 7. If you count only the professors that are actually teaching at any point in time, the ratio is 1 to 92.

"THERE YOU ARE! PENCILED IN ON THE WALL."

I'm sure we will be able to get you funding to defray your costs.

Hidden meaning: It depends on your definition of "defray." Graduate school is very expensive. Each day you will sink deeper and deeper into debt. This is compounded by the fact that while you are in school you are missing out on the opportunity to earn a real living from a regular job. So, you're getting screwed from both ends. Don't worry, it won't help. There is money available through hundreds of scholarships and fellowships. Unfortunately, you will be competing for these awards against tens of thousands of other bright and motivated students, sharply decreasing your odds of hauling in the free cash. Of course, you can take out a government loan at a reasonable interest rate. A fantastic thing about such loans is the flexibility of payment plans. In exchange for getting lower monthly payments you get more time to pay off the loan. If you stretch things out long enough you can celebrate your sixtieth birthday and your last loan payment at the same time. This flexibility, however, comes with a price. The longer the term of the loan the more you pay in interest. Thus, that $10,000 loan you took out in the year 2006, will, when it is finally paid off in 2036, have only cost you a mere $1.2 million. You can't overstate the value of a good education.

It is an exciting time to be in this field of study

Hidden meaning: My colleagues and I are searching for the next big thing in the field. The last big thing came about 15 years ago and we're currently in a "been there, done that" mode. Each year I go to two or three professional conferences with the same cast of characters, tweaking and twisting the same data to produce "novel" results. Each evening at those conferences, we all go out and have a rip-roaring time, congratulating each other on getting tenure when the field was hot. If you do discover something new and exciting, please give credit where credit is due—to me.

On your campus visit, you'll want to sit in on some classes to get a feel for the curriculum and the teaching. Here is some advice on evaluating this experience:

- **Do you have any idea what the professor is talking about?** If the answer is no, get up and leave. There's no use in getting unnecessarily depressed at this stage of the game.

- **Are the students listening in rapt attention or are their eyes glazed over?** If it is the latter, ask yourself if you could handle 12 hours of this a week without completely losing your mind? If the answer is yes, it's too late; you've already lost your mind.

- **Does the teacher speak English?** If the answer is yes, is it intelligible? Some professors have thick accents that are hard to understand, which is a definite problem in a lecture course. While many of these accents will be of foreign origin, some of the worst are homegrown. If the professor is a native of New York City or Boston, for example, watch out.

- **Is the professor really a professor?** The person in front of you may be a TA. While TA's are great in many instances, especially during labs, they should not be a major staple of your graduate education. After all, TA's are wet-behind-the-ears graduate students, as you will be soon. Do you really want to pay $30,000 a year to listen to lectures by someone like you? You're paying for the professors and you should get the professors. If they're not supposed to profess, then why are they called professors anyway?

- **Is the reading list and/or the problem set too long?** Even Evelyn Wood would have a tough time reading a thousand pages a week for one class. And Albert Einstein would be slowed by a problem set thirty deep. You wouldn't even have a chance.

Make sure you meet with students outside of class. You can tell a great deal about a program from the way they look and speak. Are they emaciated waifs, with vacant stares and big book bags weighing down their shoulders? That might be you in a couple of years. Listen to their conversation. Do they discuss the fundamental processes of the universe, the meaning of life, pluralistic democracy, quarks, or *Survivor* and *Monday Night Football?* Whatever your tastes, see if you'll fit in.

5

The Application

Doctoral applications must be approached strategically. This document is the primary means by which you are going to convince the school's Ph.D. committee to accept you. Essays are one of the most important parts of the application. While the questions may be deceptively simple, you must carefully develop your answers for maximum impact. There are different schools of thought on how to achieve this goal. Consider, for example, the following question: what are your career goals and why do you think this program can help you achieve them? You could answer with heartfelt sincerity, as a prospective empire builder, or as a beggar.

Heartfelt Sincerity

I will do my very best to become a scholar in my field and contribute mightily to the well of human knowledge from which we all must drink. As a student, I will interact every chance I get with my fellow students who, like me, are mainly interested in furthering the cause of learning....As part of this august institution of advanced education I will involve myself not only in the academic workings of the department, but also the social fabric of the campus. Through that dual role I will make significant contribution to the intellectual and cultural ambiance of the place....I am not just saying this to impress the committee, I really mean it....Scout's honor.

Prospective Empire Builder

My primary goals are clear and compelling: get a Ph.D., publish my dissertation to critical acclaim; receive a tenure track position; be the youngest assistant professor in the department's history; have a thriving consulting business on the side; get tenure; be the youngest full professor in institution's history; become known as an eminent scholar in the field; grant interviews on television; torture graduate students so that they turn out like me; and, through all of my actions, bring glory and prestige to the institution....I also plan to teach only upper-level graduate courses and have a private corner office with windows on two sides.

The Beggar

I've wanted a doctorate since I was a little girl and this is the place I've always dreamed of attending. So many of my hopes are pinned on realizing this dream that I just don't know what I'd do if next fall didn't find me part of the incoming class....I am willing to do anything if you accept me—TA two courses per semester, grade the entire department's papers, or sweep the floors. Please don't let my dreams die an agonizing death!

After putting the finishing touches on your application, it's time to mail it. Having worked so hard on the application, you will no doubt gingerly take it to the local post office and fill out the appropriate return-receipt forms so that you'll know it got to its destination. Don't be surprised if the final moments of contact with your application are the most difficult. In your hands is the document that will help determine your future. Letting go means losing control. Once the application is entrusted to the care of the United States Postal Service, it's time to wait and wonder. Better yet, go out and have a beer.

6

The Ph.D. Committee and the Selection Process

The hardest thing about waiting to hear about your application is that people you don't know are determining your fate. The members of the Ph.D. selection committee are now the most important people in your life and they know it. However much you would like to believe that you would be judged objectively, you won't be. The selection committee is made up of human beings that are as cranky, unpredictable, and subjective as you are. As they turn their attention to your application, there's no telling what thoughts will run through their minds.

It is not only the inclinations of committee members that should concern you, but also the interactions among those members. While many departments are populated with professors who get along famously, some are social units rife with discord and low-level animosity. With so many large egos floating around, and so much stock placed on developing new and competing theories and wowing one another with publication lists, it is no surprise that personality clashes happen. In the worst cases, there are professors that work down the hall from one another yet have not spoken civilly to each other in years. If some of these clashing personalities sit on the committee reviewing your application, watch out. Your application may become an intellectual football, to be batted about mercilessly until one professor or the other "wins," with winning being measured by one professor as getting you into the program, and by another professor as keeping you out.

It's not only professors who must be considered. Many Ph.D. committees have student representatives. Although such students are virtually always minority members with much less say than the professors, they do have a voice. And depending on their willingness to speak up and make good arguments they certainly can affect the outcome of the decisionmaking process.

Let's listen in on the deliberations of two Ph.D. selection committee's to see what they are all about. The first committee is the one you would hope for; they are fair and reasonable.

> **Professor Mugyridge:** Let's see, this application is for Jeremy Lundeen. He's got excellent recommendations from people that some of us on the committee know to be good judges of scholarly potential. His essay is well written. And his grades are solid. Does anyone else have anything else to add?

> **Professor Simon:** While I agree he has prepared a good application, I'm a bit concerned with the relative vagueness of his essay and goals. To say that you want to study the new frontiers in fusion and that you want to teach physics is fine and good, but is he really ready for the rigors of the dissertation? Do you get the sense that he knows what he's coming up against? It is true that the recommendations are excellent, but none of them mentions anything about his creativity and his ability to go beyond coursework to original thought.

> **Noah Swartz** (student member): I think he would fit in fine. I like the energy and enthusiasm in his essay. And, I wouldn't put too much stock in the essay's vagueness. My essay was pretty vague, and, anyway, the focus of my dissertation is not even related to what I said I wanted to do in my application.

Lundeen is accepted.

The next committee is unfair and dysfunctional.

> **Professor (Rick) Fontaine:** Mrs. Smith's biggest problem is her supporters. Her main recommendation is from Freddy Reese. Freddy is one of the least respected and least talented professors in his field. The fact that he has good things to say about Ms. Smith only works against her. And in choosing Freddy as her main advisor for her master's thesis Smith really showed poor judgment. Furthermore, she went to a second-tier university. She's not up to the standards of this institution.

Professor Taney: Rick, you say that her main recommendation is tainted because of its author. Well, does your animosity towards Reese have anything to do with his winning last year's award for the best original research from the *Journal of Pheromones and other Sexual Elixirs?* The very same award you thought you should have won? Despite your transparent pettiness, I agree that we shouldn't let Ms. Smith in. She would be a natural to work under me, but I was shocked that she didn't mention any of my pathbreaking research in her essay. She seems to be totally unaware of my major contributions to the field. That is hardly an auspicious beginning for an entering doctoral candidate.

Jane Woodward (student member): (Realizing that she is a lowly first year doctoral student taking a course with Professor Taney and is largely funded by research sponsored by Professor Fontaine, and further realizing that Ms. Smith is very impressive and would probably be a star in the department, thereby taking attention away from other students, Woodward decides that she has no choice but to say what is really on her mind). Uh, I agree. I'll be back in a second. I gotta go to the bathroom.

Smith is rejected.

7

You've Been Accepted

Go out and celebrate. Tell your family and friends. Call up that high school social studies teacher who thought you would never amount to anything and rub it in. And be sure to take a good look in the mirror. You'll see a person on the verge of one of the greatest and most intense intellectual adventures the world has to offer. If you notice a slight grimace in your visage that's just because you're beginning to fear that the horrible stories you've heard about the Ph.D. process may be true. Don't worry. In the worst case, you might lose your sense of humor, your humility, your compassion, your perspective, tens of thousands of dollars in loans and lost earning potential, and perhaps your mind. And, of course you will not get a degree and, instead will remain "All-But-Dissertation" (ABD) status for the rest of your life, a fact that you will have to explain and defend over and over again to friends and strangers alike. If you're lucky, though, you'll end up with a framed diploma, flowing robes you'll never use again, the same amount of debt, and a bound copy of your dissertation, which most likely will be read by a very small number of people. But forget all that for now and have fun. The show is about to begin.

8

Orientation Week

This orientation week is different from the one you experienced at college, where the main purpose was to make quick and fleeting friends, drink alcohol, and get lucky. Now that you're a Ph.D. student, you're more mature and less into superficial conversation and casual relationships. Instead, you go right for the alcohol. And there will be hamburgers, plenty of 'em. Indeed, there seems to be an unwritten rule that a graduate school orientation without a couple of cookouts is like a registrar's office without lines. It doesn't happen.

This is your first chance to meet your fellow students. In conversation you'll no doubt discover that although all of you are part of same species, *Homo doctoratus*, there are subspecies that have their own unique characteristics.

Homo doctoratus omniscienta

This guy has all the answers. Coursework, oral exams, and the dissertation are just formalities. He has mapped out his research questions and methodology, he knows what his findings will be, and he figures that he'll graduate in record time—three years max. Like royalty, he believes he is born to this, and he expects everyone else to treat him with deference. He laughs too loud, drops too many names, speaks in quotes, begins every sentence with "I think," and never listens. Keep an eye on this guy. It should be amusing. He'll either drop out after a year, claiming that the school is run by cretins, or be there long after you're gone, trying desperately to get some positive feedback from somebody, anybody.

Homo doctoratus confusida

She has no idea why she is here or what to expect. She has no idea what she wants to study. She has no idea why she was accepted, but figured it would be rude to turn down the school. "Anyway," she says, "school sure beats working for a living." After speaking to her, you begin to wonder about the credibility of your program's selection process and the quality of the program itself. You become confused and more nervous. It's time for another beer.

Homo doctoratus scaredshitlessa

Getting into a conversation with this subspecies can be emotionally draining.

> **You:** What do you think of that "Number Theory" course?
>
> *scaredshitlessa*: It looks hard, man, really hard. Did you see all those problem sets? They're word problems, you know, the worst kind. I prefer multiple-choice. At least you have a chance.
>
> **You:** Professor Abrams seems like a really nice guy. I think I might ask him to be my advisor.
>
> *scaredshitlessa*: I'd never do that. He's too well known. He's probably very hard to please. He'll rip you apart in your oral exams and put so much red ink on your dissertation drafts that you'll think they were murdered. He seems nice, but the nice ones are the ones you need to worry about the most.
>
> **You:** Can I get you a beer?
>
> *scaredshitlessa*: I try to avoid beer. I have an ulcer. I can tell it's going to get worse. Yes, definitely much worse.

Homo doctoratus comparativa

This person's goal in life is to figure out where she fits into the scheme of things. Her success and self-worth is measured in relation to the attributes of those around her. Since her need to compare herself to others is so strong she is always asking questions designed to size-up the competition. What college did you go to? What was your GPA? What were your SAT and GRE scores? Have you published any articles in academic journals? Her questions and motives are disturbing. The best way to deal with this type of person is to lie.

Not only did you go to the best college, but you were also *summa cum laude*. Your SAT and GRE scores are perfect and the article you just wrote is already being called an important contribution in your field. Do not offer to get her a hamburger. She is no longer hungry.

Homo doctoratus superba

She is too good to be true and almost too perfect to exist. Valedictorian of her college class, she is not only smart, but also extremely attractive. In college she led her crew team to the national championship. Rather than look down upon those around her, she is empathetic and compassionate. Her keen sense of humor has a universal appeal. She skews the class curve upward. Teachers love her. You want to hate her, but can't. She's just too nice. So, you ask her to be your lab partner and hope she accepts.

Homo doctoralus professinalissimo

This guy is a collector of degrees. He has been in academia way too long. This doctorate represents another diploma he can add to the wall. He already has two masters, a law degree, and maybe even a Ph.D. in a separate field. The campus is his womb and he doesn't wander. The elbow patches on his tweed sport jacket have patches. He is an expert on hamburgers. Odds are he is independently wealthy and/or a bit odd. But, if you have any questions about the administrative aspects the Ph.D. process, go to him for the answer. He's been there, done that.

Homo doctoratus pocketprotecto

He is identified by rumpled clothes, unkempt hair, darting eyes, cackling laugh, hunched-over bearing, thick unfashionable glasses, and a slightly earthy-musty-I'm-boycotting-anti-perspirant kind of smell. He is a true nerd, replete with a pocket-protector, a calculator on his belt, and information collection and maximization on his mind. He is likely a Trekkie and usually travels in a pack of like-minded individuals. The finer skills of social interaction are not his strong point. It is important to separate the real representatives of this subspecies from the wannabes. The single most important distinguishing feature is intelligence. The true nerds are actually very smart. The wannabes just act that way. They are pseudo-intellectuals. Avoid wannabes at all costs. And, whatever you do, never have one for a lab partner.

HOMO DOCTORATUS
PROFESSIONALISSIMO

HOMO DOCTORATUS
CONFUSIDA

HOMO DOCTORATUS
POCKET PROTECTO

Homo doctoratus hypotheoso

She has a desperate need to explain everything with a theory, and every theory is based on a set of hypotheses that need testing. She is not interested in what actually happens, but what is likely to happen given the proper alignment of twenty-seven variables. To her the world is a tentative place that has to be tested to be understood. Causal connections are everywhere, waiting to be found. A beautiful theory is much better than messy reality. Shit happens is never a good enough explanation. Avoid eating out with this person. Even ordering food can be an in-depth analytical exercise, rife with alternative outcomes that must be balanced and weighed. If romance is on your mind, beware. She is always searching for the null hypothesis, and the problem is, you might fit the bill.

Homo doctoratus workaholica

Enough is never enough for this person. There is always one more source to consult, one more problem set to conquer, one more case study to evaluate. He is often driven as much by the love of learning as the fear of failure or being uncovered as an academic lightweight. Twenty-four hour libraries are his temples, the Internet his salvation, and study groups his preferred form of community. Accuse him of being a workaholic and he will deny it. Then, he will excuse himself and get back to work.

Fortunately, most of your fellow doctoral students will be fairly normal, like you. Use the orientation week to get to know them and make sure you go to as many cookouts and catered gatherings as possible. You'll have plenty of time to become a starving graduate student later. But make sure to avoid filling your pockets with food unless you're not seen. First impressions are very important.

9

Classes

Many, if not most, Ph.D. programs require a couple of years of classes before you can take your general exams, which are commonly called preliminary exams (prelims) or qualifying exams. This requirement often holds even if you have just completed two years of master's classes in the same discipline. If you're like me, your response to this situation is something like "hey, what the hell is going on? I've just finished two years of courses and you want two more, and then add to that another four to six years working through the general exams and the dissertation. Are you people crazy?" Actually, while this is what I thought, what I said at the time was "gee, two more years of learning and intellectual growth, sounds exciting."

The coursework requirement will not come as a surprise. The school brochures will inform you about the hurdles you have to overcome on the way to the doctorate. Still, it may lead you to wonder why you got a master's degree in the first place if it places you in pretty much the same place as someone entering the Ph.D. program right after college or after working for a number of years. In my case, the answer was clear. My department all but required applicants to have a master's degree to be seriously considered.

The first piece of advice for selecting classes is don't believe everything you read. Course descriptions can sound exciting while the course itself might stink. After all, the course description is one of the primary means the professor has to reel you in. If the course is bad, he's not going to admit that. However independent professors are, the university or college still requires them to attract students; no students, no course. The fewer the number of courses, the more unhappy the students. The more unhappy the students, the more unhappy the administration. And the more unhappy the administration, the more uncomfortable the professor. Of course, there are undoubtedly some places where no matter how unhappy the students are, things will never change. But even those places will eventually reap what they sow and lose stature or possibly go out of business. In a time of budget cutting and declining enrollments, institutions of higher learning are becoming more attuned to the need to sell their product. And the most important purchaser is you, the student. Your tuition dollars are paying a good part of your professor's salaries. You are entitled to demand as much from them as they demand from you. Never forget that. You're not a peon, you're the boss.

Back to the classes. To give you an idea of the potential disparity between words and reality, consider the following:

Political Science 345—The Politics of Protest: The 1960s and the Remaking of America

What the course catalogue says:

The decade began with unbridled optimism and ended with despair and the deep division of American society. What force, in the course of ten short years, could shake the foundations of government and lead people, of all walks of life, to question their belief systems and what it means to be an American? The answer is protest. We will explore the transformation of the New Frontier and the Great Society into a cultural battlefield. Meet the images and voices of nuclear annihilation, the civil rights movement, Vietnam, flower power, and middle-class America. Learn how mass movements begin and are sustained, how leaders lead, how passions flare and fade, and how the "system" copes with attacks from without and within. Tune into the sixties and get turned on to the most pivotal decade in the post World War II era.

What the course is really like:

Professor Longley lived through the sixties, a fact he will remind you of ad nauseam. In his eyes, you young punks are vapid, MTV-bred, generation-Xers, who suck at the teat of capitalism and are more interested in taking than giving back to society. The only cause he thinks you're willing to fight for is freedom of speech, but this puzzles him since he knows you have nothing important to say. He doesn't like you, and you won't like him. To make matters worse, Professor Longley is still tripping after all these years. At least twice a month he jets off to some conference of aging hippie/academics, who talk about, what else, how important the sixties are and how subsequent generations sold their souls to the almighty dollar. In Longley's absence, his teaching assistant, who is of your generation but has learned to loathe himself under Longley's tutelage, will monotonically read to you from the notes the Professor left behind. When Longley is in town, he too reads from his notes, punctuating his melodramatic delivery with stories from the frontlines the revolution, e.g., "when I was marching hand-in-hand with Martin...," "when I was being bitten by a police-dog in Watts...," "when I placed a daisy in the barrel of soldier's gun in front of the Pentagon..." Professor Longley's hatred of materialistic society may strike you as especially hypocritical. He drives a Range Rover, lives in a $600,000 house, repeatedly speed-dials his broker throughout the day, and sends his children to prep school. We think he doth protest too much.

Although appearances might deceive, there are other more useful ways to select courses. Start off by asking your advisor for advice. After all, that's why he gets the big bucks, and he has undoubtedly heard numerous comments from students about which courses are good and which are bad. Then talk to students who have taken the course in recent years. They'll let you know whether the lectures are the human-equivalent of Valium or the Sermon on the Mount. Also, talk to the professor. Interview her for the job of teaching you.

Once you have picked six, seven, or maybe eight classes, go shopping. Sit in on each one to get a perspective on the professor and the course material. Then choose three or four of the courses, and jettison the rest. Although shopping around is usually encouraged, many students don't take advantage of this excellent selection tool. In my case, I sometimes chose courses based on time slots and not quality. I liked to have entire days without classes, and in order to accommodate my desire I picked four strategically-placed courses, and stuck with them. In hindsight, shopping more would have been a good idea, even if it meant having courses spread throughout the week. Of course, some doctoral programs require students to take specific courses taught by specific professors with no opportunity to shop and choose. In that case, hope for the best.

In your classes you will encounter your peers. They come in all types. Watch and listen. Soon you will be able to tell them apart on the basis of their salient characteristics. In the corner you will notice a student who is sloppily dressed, unshaven, never takes notes, never asks questions, often cradles his head in the crook of his arm, and has a wealth of facial expressions, all of which seem to say "big deal." Don't be deceived. This guy is no dunce. He won't pull down the class's average. Rather he will probably get the highest grade. His intellect is so keen that he is able to flout convention and conformity yet still absorb and understand more than you do in half the time. There is the chance, however, that the person fitting this description is actually going to be a poor student, a slug, or a near-do-well. No theory is right every time.

Then there is the questioner. She seems to feel it is her duty to explore all issues to the fullest. The questions are often excellent; ones you wished you had asked yourself. But, as the semester progresses, asking questions for her becomes a habit that can't be broken, and if she runs out of interesting questions she'll replace them with the mundane or the maddening. "The reading list says pages 20 to 35 this week. Next week it is 37 to 55. What about 36?" Or "that derivative is highly interesting, do you think it sheds any light on the meaning of life?" A variation on the questioner is the pontificator. He raises his hand ostensibly to ask a question, but when called upon gives a mini-lecture, designed to impress the class and teacher, but which never evolves into an actual question.

10

Outside of Class

As a graduate student you will become extremely familiar with the library. Your hands will fly, with deft assurance over the computerized catalogue keyboards, searching out academic minutia, all in an effort to write the most amazing, pithy, and knowledgeable papers ever seen in the halls of your great institution. But your life has to extend beyond the stacks and carrels and the stagnant, often fetid air that accompanies the accumulation of the tens of thousands of books that haven't been cracked open for years. To the pub and the coffee shops ye must go. There you can relax, meet with friends, discuss world affairs and, more often than not, dish on your program and your professors.

Watch out for the espresso drinkers. There is evidence that extensive espresso drinking indicates a desire to avoid reality. With each cup the drinker becomes more profound. The head slumps. The sentences become longer and more incomprehensible. The pull of the bean sucks them into the realm of irrelevance. They are so caffeinated that time loses all meaning. The faster they talk the smarter they feel. Do yourself a favor. Drink your coffee straight up, or better yet, decaffeinated. That way you'll remain in control of your senses and capable of making it to the bathroom in time to avoid embarrassment.

Take advantage of the pubs and cafes. Graduate school is a great place to just hang out and have fun. At least until you begin your dissertation research and start pulling your hair out and wondering if it's too late to…. But that will have to wait until later in the book. In the meantime, attend classes, play with theoretical constructs, eat, drink, and be merry.

11

Buying Books

As a doctoral student you will buy many books. Sometimes a class requires only a single book. For example, the tenth edition of Smiggeldorf's Current Geology. You could borrow this book from the library instead of buying it, but if you try to you will quickly discover that either the book is already checked out by the professor or another student, or the only edition the library has is the first, which is so old that it contains a debate on the new theory of plate tectonics. Other courses will require you to buy many books. It will be equally difficult to find these in the library, so, inevitably, whatever courses you take, you will have to go to the university bookstore and spend money.

If you're lucky, the required books will be in paperback, in the used book section, and already excellently annotated by other students who have taken the course in previous years. Paperbacks are cheaper than hardcovers, and used paperbacks are cheaper than new ones. But the piece de resistance of this Triple Crown of book buying is in the annotations. Good annotations not only can give you insights into the most important parts of the book, by virtue of highlighting, but they can also provide insights that go beyond the written text, assuming that the former owner took the time to write their comments and thoughts in the margins. This is useful only if the former owner of the book was also a good and conscientious student. The musings of a student who got a C in the class are not of much use. Worse, are students who plant fake insights in the margins just to throw you off. This is one of the most heinous crimes a student can commit within the confines a doctoral program. Lying to professors is one thing, but misleading another student, that is treachery most foul. I have no evidence that doctoral students actually have stooped so low, but, still, it behooves you to be cautious. Gaze upon annotations in textbooks with suspicious eyes.

Since you graduated from college and, very likely, have one graduate degree to your credit, the exorbitant price of many textbooks will come as no surprise. However, because you are now taking courses that cover ever more obscure and specific topics, some of the books you must buy will be ridiculously expensive. The main reason for this is that the market for highly specialized books is often very small. For example, you and 12 other people might be the only ones to purchase a copy of Wagstaff's Theories of Capillary Function in the Constricted Spaces of Titmouse Duodenums. The publisher has to recoup the costs for producing this expensive tome, and the only hope of doing so is to charge an outrageous price. So, don't take it personally. Indeed, one could imagine a course so specialized that it is only offered at your university, and the only book for the course is the one written by the professor, and the only people that buy the book are the 4 to 6 students that take it each year. You might have to shell out $200 for that one! Whatever you do, don't tell the professor of this course your theories on captive audiences and academic extortion.

In the early years of your doctoral program, you will likely have a manageable number of books. A single bookcase should be able to hold them. As the years mount, so too will the number of books. You can always buy more bookcases, but you might run out of space, especially if you have been spending so much on books that you only have enough money left over to pay for rice cakes, milk, and a one-room efficiency in the inexpensive part of town. There are two other alternatives. You can stack the books creatively around your apartment. A pile of urban planning books makes quite a nice nightstand. And all those engineering books could be incorporated into a winning coffee table design. Another option is to sell some of your books back to the bookstore. But, don't get your hopes up.

The worst thing about purchasing books is that they are one of the most rapidly depreciating assets known to humankind. The moment you buy a new textbook, it looses roughly half its value. You will discover this should you ever decide to sell it back to the bookstore at the end of the semester. Even if you've never cracked the binding nor curled a page, it is still a used book and its value is set accordingly. The bookstore's willingness to buy back your books, of course, is contingent on more than just its condition; the books also have to be current. Many textbooks are updated and new editions printed on a regular basis, perhaps every couple of years. Unless you are selling the current edition of the book, the bookstore is not going to want it because all the new students are required to buy the edition that came after the one you have. In that event, your book is virtually worthless. Therefore, if you want to get some of your investment back, it is best to sell your books as soon as you have no need for them. If you wait too long, the chance to sell will pass you by. But even this strategy will fail if publishers and authors become delirious and, in an effort sell more books, start pumping out new editions every semester. Then, the only economically rational choice you will have is to get into the academic publishing business, fast.

If neither the creative piling of books nor selling them to the bookstore works for you, there is another option. You can throw the books in the recycling bin. This is not recommended. After spending so much money on books, you might be loath to just toss them out. This will certainly be the case if the money you spent is not yours, but was supplied by your parents or the government. After all, someday you might need to prove that you used the money for your education. Still, if you have no choice but to get the books out of your apartment try composting them and using the compost as fertilizer for your plants, instead of throwing the books in the garbage. That way you will at least get something in return. Your plants will be healthier and smarter, and you will lend new meaning to the term "sunk costs."

12

The Appearance of Work

Many doctoral students are able to concentrate for hours on end while reading, researching, and writing. They rush to the library, sit down at a carrel, and start working. When they get up six hours later to leave the library, they have actually done six hours worth of real work. They also have amazingly strong bodily control, being able to sit that long without a bathroom break. Most doctoral students are not like this. For them an hour of pure concentration and laser-like purpose would be an intellectual miracle. They need distraction. More importantly, they need to feel like they are really working hard when in fact they are wasting a lot of time. Appearances are equally important to these people, so they also need to look like they are really working hard as opposed to hardly working. If you fall into this category, here is some advice that should enable you to achieve such lofty goals.

The first key is to know when to start the clock. If you want to go to the library to study, do not simply count the hours you spend in the library, also count the time it takes you to get to and from the facility. To feel intellectually honest about doing so, make sure that you think about studying at least once during every twenty-minute period that you spend in transit. If you are thinking particularly weighty thoughts, you can extend that to once every thirty minutes. Of course, this tactic gives unfair advantage to those who live farther away from the library. There are ways, however, to counteract this. If you live within a few minutes of the library, you can move further out. If that is too draconian a step, you can simply be more creative in getting to the library. There are undoubtedly many routes you can take. Try a different one each day to see which one suits you best and which one gives you the amount of intellectual credit you seek. And don't worry about direction. There is no rule that says you have to walk toward the library. Start out in the opposite direction if you like and turn around when you damn well please. Just make sure you keep thinking about your work every twenty or thirty minutes. That will sustain you.

Once you are at the library, begin scouting for a seat. This could take anywhere from a couple of minutes to a half-hour, depending on how you do it. If you want to sit down quickly because your feet are tired from too much walking, then just take the first seat you find. If, on the other hand, you still have some fight left in you, then the first thing you should do is circumnavigate the entire library. Every good doctoral student knows that you have to be conversant with the literature before you can decide what theories to apply and what arguments to make or experiments to run. Well, the same goes for finding a seat. If you don't know all the options, how will you know that you are making a wise choice? The bigger the library, the more time you can kill. And don't forget to do some reconnaissance in the basement, an often overlooked piece of real estate that just might have some chairs, and perhaps a couple of decomposed doctoral students whose library cards expired years ago.

As soon as you sit down, take time to arrange your books. Then go to the bathroom. Even if you don't have to go, take the opportunity to see how you look. Because the better you look, the better you feel, and the better you feel, the less guilt you will have taking so much time to do so little. But I digress. After you come back from the bathroom, sit and ponder for a while. Think about what you would like to accomplish today. Think about all the other students all over the United States who are getting doctorates in your field. Think about them sitting at their library desks thinking just like you. Then, start thinking one step ahead of them so that you will get your degree before they do and, thereby, beat them to that perfect job you've always dreamed of. Procrastination is not only a fine art; it is one that requires you to think strategically. You can waste time, but only to a point.

Now, open one of your books and begin reading. Every time you see a footnote, read it. If the footnote cites other works, write them down. And before you read any further, you must get up and go to the computer catalog, get the call numbers for the cited materials, and then track them down in the stacks. Once you have retrieved all the works cited in the first footnote, you have to evaluate what the author of your book has said in light of the original sources. You need to check the quality of the scholarship. You cannot simply assume that the author has used the footnoted materials properly, especially if you want to use information from the book in question. After all, once you write something the liability is yours. You cannot pawn your problems off on others even if they provided you with false information. You must be absolutely intellectually meticulous and beyond reproach.

Once you have satisfied yourself that the author of the book you are reading has used the sources cited in this first footnote properly, you can continue reading. If you are reading the work of another scholar such as yourself, no doubt there will be numerous footnotes (see more on this in Chapter 22). In that case, it will be hours, perhaps days, before you get through the first couple of pages. That would be splendid wouldn't it, because all the while you could rightfully claim to be doing real work. Do try, however, to stay away from books that smack of the popular. They are often skimpily footnoted and, therefore, offer little traction for the serious doctoral student.

It is important to note, lest you be too zealous, that there are limits to checking. No matter how much you might want to rack up more time, there is no need to check the footnotes of works cited in the footnotes of the work you are reading. The virtue of doing so is that eventually you would dig deep enough to find the original source for a particular idea, theory, or thought. You would get to the point where there are simply no more footnotes to pursue. And you would uncover the horrible truth that everything of any importance in the world can actually be traced to a guy named Bernie who lived in Mesopotamia in 7000 BC. But, alas that would take too long. You'd be at it for years. So, stop at the first level of intellectual suspicion and move on.

While you are checking footnotes, be on the lookout for other opportunities to extend the sense that you are doing real work. The copying machine offers one such opportunity. Perhaps you need a copy of one of the sources. Go for it and rack up more intellectual capital (see the next chapter for a more in-depth discussion of copying and the risks it entails). While you are at the copy machine, make sure to visit the water fountain and take in deep draughts of cold, clear refreshment. The more you drink, the sooner you will have to take a bathroom break, and, well, you know that strategy already.

When you tire of reading, stroll over to the computerized catalog and do a search for everything ever written on your subject of study. Make sure you access every database the library has, and if you can get to the Internet, go there and search, search, search. You might be thinking, after you've done this once, why would you need to do it again? How naïve you are. The font of wisdom and learning is constantly bubbling, and to keep up with it you need to dip your nose into the waters on a regular basis. Every week there are new items added to databases and the web sites. How will you know if they are critical to your work, unless you look? And just think, a thorough search could take you hours.

It's about time to wrap things up for the day. You've been at the library for many hours and feel as if you've done a lot of work. Better yet, all the other people who saw you at the library think you did a lot of work. Now, gather your belongings. Stretch your legs for the journey home. And don't forget to go to the bathroom.

13

The Copying Game

At first the desire will be weak. You'll copy an article here, a couple of pages there. As time wears on the pull will grow stronger. You'll purchase a $20 copying card and start spending half an hour a day reproducing. It will become an obsession. No article will be too obscure, no book chapter too lengthy to subject to the magic light. Hour upon hour of copying will not satisfy your craving for more knowledge. You'll become an expert at clearing jams, replacing toner, and un-crinkling currency so it can be fed into the card machine with unceasing regularity. Your apartment will become an obstacle course, with columns of paper reaching up to the ceiling. Surveying all that you have duplexed, collated, and stapled, you will become swept up in a vortex of intellectual bliss, feeling as one with all the scholars whose works you have brought into your life and laid at your feet.

The only problem is that most of the material you copied you will never read, and fifty percent of what you do read is not interesting anyway. What doctoral students too often fail to realize is that copying is one of the highest forms of procrastination. At first you'll read documents and then copy them so as to have a ready reference for later use. Next, you'll skim them before copying. Then you'll simply note the title of the paper or chapter, and seeing that it has something to do with your research, copy it. In this fashion, copying becomes a surrogate for the actual work and thought required to read text and absorb its lessons. With the pile labeled, "to be read," growing bigger all the time, the disconnect between what you know and what you think you know increases. You'll assume that the bigger your bibliography the better, but without an understanding of your bibliography's contents, it will be nothing more than a waste of space.

Be selective. For any subject, there's always more information out there than you can absorb or even copy. The best doctoral students are the ones who conserve their time, energy, and money by not confusing quantity with quality.

"CONGRATULATIONS! YOU'RE THE FIRST
STUDENT TO HAVE EVER USED
A TON OF TONER."

14

You Can't Eat Words

Some doctoral students are lucky enough to actually pay for school and living expenses without borrowing money or having a job. They can afford to be students, period. Most students, however, are not so fortunate. If you fall into this latter category, you will have to work or take out massive loans to pay your bills and buy food, and most likely you will have to do both. Many people argue that putting yourself through school, with a combination of loans and jobs, builds character. That might be true, but it also builds fatigue and debt. My advice to you is, if you can swing it, be born rich.

With respect to part-time jobs, you will probably have opportunities to work in your field, either in a lab, on a project, or with a local organization or company. Alternatively, you could get a job that has nothing to do with what you're studying. There is no right or wrong path. But before deciding, ask three basic questions. First, do you have any rich relatives whose assistance could keep you from having to work? Second, does the job offer a 401(k)? And third, will the job help you get dates? Once you have evaluated the answers to these questions, you will be ready to make a reasoned choice.

While jobs come and go, loans are forever, or nearly so. That is why you must proceed cautiously when racking up debt. The pernicious thing about loans is that while you're in school, you don't really experience them. You fill out an application, get the money for a split second, hand it over to the bursar, and then don't hear about it until after you graduate, when payments begin. This delayed impact often lulls students into a false sense of security. And because one loan is rarely enough, students who have out-of-sight-out-of-mind mentality when it comes to borrowing money can be quite surprised by the bill that is presented to them on the heels of graduation day. As with picking a job, before taking out loans one must ask three questions. First, are you likely to marry a rich person who believes that outstanding loans are a social faux pas that must be immediately rectified? Second, would you consider going to school forever so you never have to pay off the loans? And third, what are your feelings about the Internal Revenue Service?

"THERE YOU HAVE IT. THE WORLD'S OLDEST MAN ACHIEVED HIS LIFELONG DREAM OF OUTLIVING HIS STUDENT LOAN PAYMENTS."

15

Picking a Committee

In many departments the Ph.D. committee is formed prior to your general exams. This is so you and your committee can work together in crafting the content of the exam and ensuring that you are properly prepared. The committee grades your exam, and if there is an oral defense they administer it. In other departments, the general exam is more of a communal activity, with all doctoral students in the same cohort facing the same set of questions at the same time. In this case, the committee is usually not formed until the start of the dissertation. For those whose committee forms after the exams, you can come back to this section after reading the next chapter on the "big test."

In an ideal world your Ph.D. committee would be three or four brilliant people who are sages in your field and have read and seen just about everything and therefore are well equipped to steer you through the minefields involved in passing your general exams and finishing the dissertation. They will listen intently to your concerns and ideas, offer good counsel, be available when you need them, and provide support when times get rough. Well, if you're fortunate this is the way it will be. More commonly, your committee, no matter how good it is, will be lacking in certain areas. If you're unlucky you'll have the committee from hell whose main entertainment is alternately ignoring and castigating you.

Just as with picking schools, there are various theories about picking a Ph.D. committee. Your decision should be based on one or more of the following:

Notoriety

Here the goal is to get the biggest names in your school and your field on the committee. Just being associated with such transcendent beings will raise your stock. If you get along with these intellectual titans and impress them with your scholarship, they will open doors to your future. A recommendation from a luminary has an amazing impact on lesser mortals. Similarly, constructive criticism from such minds can be more valuable than reading a hundred books on your topic. You can benefit from their learning and avoid mistakes.

One potential drawback of having committee members like this is that it might be very difficult to get their attention. After all, plenty of other people are clamoring for their time. You might have to wait your turn. Another thing to watch out for is the ego factor. If your committee members are in possession of enormous egos and fond of intellectual battle, you could be reduced to a pulpy mass of fleshy matter in short order unless you are secure enough to withstand the assault the members will undoubtedly launch in your direction.

Obscurity

The opposite of notoriety is obscurity. Virtually every department has professors who are relatively minor names in their field. They may have tenure but that fact just causes everyone to question the validity of the tenure system. Their research is mediocre. Placing such people on your committee may enable you to underachieve and still graduate. There is always the chance that because they didn't or weren't able to push themselves intellectually, they may take the same approach with you. And if you are actually a deeper thinker than they are, your best effort will certainly be good enough for them. This path, however, can be fraught with peril if these individuals are bitter about their academic shortcomings and choose to take it out on you. Few things are worse than the vengeance of a depressed and unfulfilled individual.

Dominance

The most important member of the committee is the chairperson. She organizes the other members, communicates most closely with the student, and exerts the greatest influence on the outcome of the Ph.D. process. In some cases, the chairperson is so dominant that all the members defer to her and the committee becomes a de-facto dictatorship. If you get along with the chairperson, then selecting a dominant one could be a good choice. Instead of multiple audiences, you can focus on pleasing her. If, on the other hand, the relationship between you and the chairperson becomes rocky, dealing with your committee will become pure hell. Because of the chairperson's dominance you cannot turn to other committee members for effective support. You're on your own in a situation typified by asymmetrical power in which you have very little.

Compatibility

Committees usually act in a consensual manner. In the end they have to agree before you pass your general exam and dissertation. One way to help forge agreement is to make sure the members get along. This way they can engage each other constructively rather than destructively. Because they are familiar and enjoy one another's company it should be easier to get them to communicate and convene in one room. Friendliness or, at least, professional respect and cordiality among committee members goes a long way towards heading off problems before they arise.

If, on the other hand, your committee members can't stand each other or each other's ideas and pet theories, you may end up being a ball they bat around while working through their angst and anger. No matter how good are their minds or their individual advice, it is hard to progress if you can't get your committee to meet, discuss, and help you work through the difficulties of the Ph.D. process.

To illustrate the importance of the committee consider the following two true stories. In one, the Ph.D. student in question got along famously with his committee, especially his chairman. Committee meetings were times of academic bonhomie and intellectual jocularity. He knew his committee member's families and was often joined his professors for a beer or something to eat. His dissertation defense was tough but fair and very civil. With degree in hand, his committee members went out of their way to network on behalf of their student and they did indeed help him secure a good job. To this day, he still communicates with his committee members. He is truly one of their peers.

Another Ph.D. I know had a totally different experience. Things got ugly fast. His committee failed to make much effort to coordinate amongst themselves or with him. It was a constant struggle for him to get time with them. When he did get their attention, all he got was a lecture about the failures of his research to date. Making matters worse was the animosity that two members had towards one another. When they were in the room together sparks flew and the student got singed. The relationship between the chairperson and the student got so bad that they nearly came to blows and for a year couldn't bear to be in the same room together. He finally graduated and has not seen or contacted any of his committee members since.

The message here is that you must pick wisely. Your committee has a major influence on the quality or your work and the likelihood that you'll graduate. Interview potential committee members. Find out what is important to them and how they view the committee process. A little bit of advance work can help you avoid a whole lot of pain and trauma.

"AFTER PROFESSOR SAMUELS SAID 'IS TOO' PROFESSOR HASTINGS SAID 'IS NOT.'"

16

The Big Test

No one knows why the exams that allow you to proceed to the dissertation phase of your doctorate are called general exams. Mine certainly were not general. They asked very specific questions that you could only answer if you had taken very specific courses that taught you very specific things. The average Joe, right off the street, could not have passed my general exams. I didn't even pass my general exams the first time, and various people, including myself, had already invested over $150,000 in my post-secondary education.

Every graduate school has a different routine. Some have three-hour exams where all the students taking the exam have to answer the same set of questions. Others have more onerous obstacles to overcome. In my case, the general exam consisted of five questions that I had five days to answer. It was open book and each answer was supposed to be 10 pages, double-spaced, or less. Before I got the questions, I thought I would have little problem. After all, it was open book and I had over 100 relevant books in my room. Also, my professors knew what courses I had taken and what I knew. The questions would be hard but I was sure I could handle them.

Was I ever wrong. I took one look at the questions and panicked. They wanted to know how I would resolve specific policy questions. The problem was so did I. Each day, for each question, I argued with myself and stayed up later and later. The books didn't help. None of the authors seemed to agree. If they couldn't agree, I wondered, how could I come up with THE answer? It wasn't fair. To make matters worse, my girlfriend stayed over one night. I shared all my insecurities and her only response was "you're a loser." This was not my idea of good foreplay and I went to sleep. She left the next morning and I attacked the remaining questions with the vigor of a wet noodle. Nothing I typed made sense.

Finally, I handed in my completed exam and went home to eat a pint of ice cream and call my family to tell them I was a failure. Unfortunately, none of them would accept the charges and I was left alone to mope in a puddle of chocolate goo.

The next week the committee chairman called me into his office. I've got good news and bad news. Which do you want first? Give me the good news first, I said. Okay, life will go on. What is the bad news I asked? Well, he said, taking in a deep breath, you're answers really sucked. Well, he actually said it more gently than that, but I knew what he meant. I slumped into my chair and saw my life flash before my eyes. Years from now I would be a beggar telling people I could have been a doctor, but for my tragic flaw—I couldn't prove a hypothesis. In fact, I didn't have a clue.

My professors had different opinions on how to react to this situation. The chairman wanted me to regroup by leaving school for a few months and take the exams again when I returned. He was confident that I was capable of not only passing, but also of completing a good dissertation. He fought to have me admitted into the program and didn't particularly want one of "his" students flunking out. Another professor on my committee got right to the point. "Maybe," he said, "you're just not cutout to be an academic. You like writing, why don't you become a professional writer? Cut your losses and get on with life." However heartfelt his advice I couldn't take it. If there's one group of people more pitiful than struggling Ph.D. students, it's struggling writers.

I wanted to act positive, work hard, take the exams again, and pass with flying colors. But, like so many people who have faced failure squarely in the eye, I felt lousy. For days I wandered around in haze until I decided the only thing that could be more painful than taking the exams again was giving up. This is not to say that there aren't good and valid reasons for dropping out of a Ph.D. program, even after you've invested a number of years; there are and they are considered in a later chapter. It's just that in my case, giving up was not an acceptable option.

Over the next couple of months my professors gave me practice questions that I answered and had critiqued. I got better. My answers became stronger. My confidence increased. And then E-Day arrived. I picked up my second general exam and went home to work. It came much easier this time and I passed. The next day I noticed it was spring.

If you talk to people about their experience going through their general exams you will get different stories. I know of people who wrote fantastic answers and flew through their oral exams without a hitch. These are the same people who have color-coded sock drawers and know how many cups are in a quart. But there are many doctoral students who didn't have it so easy. One guy I heard about really knew his stuff but got very nervous during his orals. Although he had written compelling answers, when his professors asked him to elaborate he was struck mute. Minutes went by and he said nothing. His fears had paralyzed his mind. His professors, understanding souls that they were, passed him and immediately repaired to a local bar where they belted down a few. Not surprisingly, the student then had little problem communicating.

Based on my experience and the experiences of many others, the best advice I can offer for taking general exams is this. Make sure your significant other is sympathetic, avoid cable television, use big words, cite your professor's work, and don't eat a pint of chocolate ice cream out of the container on a white couch. Oh yeah, I forgot the most important thing—you've got to know what the hell you're talking about. After all, a Ph.D. ain't chopped liver.

17

The Dissertation Proposal

With your general exams behind you, time has come to figure out what topic you are going to spend years and years studying so that you can write an authoritative and persuasive dissertation. To make your task easier, rule out all-encompassing topics that would be worthy of Aristotle. For example, uncovering the meaning of life is not narrow enough. Nor is discovering a hitherto unknown subatomic particle. Instead, focus on manageable topics like "variations in the molecular configuration of pavement samples taken from exit ramps off of interstate 95 in New Jersey," or "how to negotiate your way out of a paper bag by creating a 'win-win' situation for you and the bag." Your dissertation may not be earth shattering, but that's okay. Just remember that the best dissertation is one that's done, and that the true purpose of the dissertation is to get you out of graduate school, the sooner the better. Who cares if nobody reads it? A finished and bound dissertation looks damn impressive and makes an effective doorstop.

Researching and writing the dissertation is a totally different experience from taking classes and your general exam. This is the beginning of the "lonely" time. No, you will not be truly alone. Your professors will meet with you occasionally, you'll still have friends, still do things that normal people do, but in the end, it's all up to you. That can be really lonely and scary.

The first thing that will and should make you nervous is the fundamental premise of the dissertation process—originality. Your research is supposed to contribute something new to the world. This is not a big book report. You can't simply interview people and relate what they said. Having a sort of interesting idea won't do. You need to come up with something new and to approach a question in a way that nobody else has. That's hard.

If you're scared now, that's okay; many people are at this point. Here is some perspective that will help you succeed. Don't place too much importance on your dissertation. It won't be your crowning achievement. While the dissertation will undoubtedly be your most important intellectual accomplishment to date, you'll move onto bigger and better things. Wouldn't it be depressing if your dissertation turned out to be your best piece of academic scholarship? This is just the first stage of your career. The dissertation's primary goal is to teach you how to pose good questions and then solve them. It is the exercise through which you gain the tools necessary to continue learning and adding to the body of knowledge for years to come. It's an apprenticeship. To become a master will take years. So go easy on yourself. Work hard, but don't allow better to always be the enemy of good enough. Most dissertations are forgettable; not for you, of course, but as far as the rest of the world goes. Just remember that Minerva's Owl flies at dusk, meaning that wisdom comes with age. The dissertation is a beginning, not an end. The sooner you realize that, the easier the journey will be.

Now that you've put things in perspective, here's some more information that will make writing your proposal easier. You can always change course on your dissertation and probably will. Before I was through I'd gone through three dissertation topics and written over 400 pages of drafts that died. At one point my professors were so concerned about my level of output-without-progress that they commanded me to stop writing and think about what I wanted to say. One professor actually held up about 200 pages of one of my drafts, which constituted only two of eight planned chapters, and declared "there's no way in hell I'm going to read an 800 page dissertation!" If you get a professor who is as straightforward as this one, you'll be lucky. He was right. During the early stages of my dissertation I suffered from the belief that bulk could make up for content. The more doubts I had about my work, the more I wrote. The folly of my efforts only became clear to me after I successfully defended my dissertation. That day I walked into the spare bedroom in our apartment, which served as the "dissertation lair," and for the first time realized that much of the space was taken up by earlier drafts of my various dissertations. I filled up a 1987 Honda Civic getting that mass of paper delivered to recycling bins at my school. Recycling still gives me the chills.

"SORRY, BUT I THINK I MIGHT HAVE ACCIDENTALLY FILLED THE PAPER TOWEL DISPENSER WITH YOUR DISSERTATION PAPERS."

Before preparing your dissertation proposal, take a small vacation or do something else that makes you feel good. You've just passed the most important test of your life and it's time to celebrate and clear your head. A week or a month break will not kill your momentum, no matter what anyone says. If you think the process leading up to the general exam was grueling, you haven't seen anything yet. Before you depart for your self-guided journey through the intellectual wilderness, relax a bit. You'll be positioned that much better to get the job done. I took this advice a bit to an extreme. After passing my general exam, I didn't focus on my dissertation proposal for six months. Instead, I worked a couple of jobs to make money, went to a lot of movies, and tried desperately to get dates!

To prepare your proposal you must decide what interests you. What questions make you say "I'd really like to know the answer to that?" or "that's interesting?" Without this type of reaction you will never be able to write a good dissertation, and the odds are you won't even be able to finish. To see why, think about the future. You have to write a significant piece of work. You have to do a lot of research. That all takes time, lots of it. If you're not interested in your topic now, just think how bored you'll be two, three, or eight years from now when you have to bring the doctorate to closure. If the topic doesn't really excite you at the outset, forget it. I know what you're thinking. The really interesting topics focus on the big questions, not the manageable, narrow ones of the type most doctoral students pursue. So how can you reconcile the need to be manageable with the need to be highly interesting? Good question. You figure it out; you're the one getting the Ph.D.

One way to determine whether your topic is worth the fight is to discuss it with friends and family. If you find it difficult to tell them what it is you want to study and why, then that's a good sign that you're going down the wrong path. Similarly, if your description of what it is you want to do puts your friends and family to sleep, consider another approach. Some might say this latter piece of advice is off the mark. After all, not all research can be exciting to the average person. Of course that's true. Yet, if you are unable to make your friends and family see even a glimmer of what it is you find so interesting, or at least infect them with your enthusiasm for the topic, the best advice is proceed with caution. It may turn out that you're just so far ahead of everyone else that it is they, not you, who have the poor judgment. There is also a good chance that you will find out your friends and family have a good deal of common sense and that you ignored them at your peril.

Another key to a successful dissertation proposal is communication and feedback. The professors on your committee work for you. You pay part of their salary and if it weren't for you and your peers they would be out of a job. Don't let the fact that they know a lot more than you make you scared to ask them questions about your direction and progress. If your professors are good then this will be easy. You won't have to beg for their time and advice. They will demand that you keep them apprised of your progress on a regular basis, and they will seek to help you in any way they can. Keep in mind, however, that often the best way to help someone work through a problem is to not give them the answer, but to give them the minimal amount of direction necessary to let them figure out the problem on their own. If, on the other hand, getting help from one or more of your professors is like pulling teeth, kick them off your committee if you can. Some schools have strict requirements about committee membership where such an action might not be allowed. But if your school is like mine, then it is you who pick the committee and you who can change it with cause. This is your education so take charge of it. Also, don't forget to take advantage of your peers. Fellow doctoral students, especially those that have gone through this process, can offer perspective, advice, and support. It might even be a good idea to start a dissertation proposal working group so you can share ideas on a regular basis.

Here is one last piece of advice about the dissertation proposal. Even if you are absolutely sure of your topic and the approach you plan to take, don't work and work and work on your proposal until it is a perfect roadmap to years of research. While it behooves you to make the proposal as strong as possible, perfection or completeness is not only a foolish goal, it subverts the very basis of the research, which is the glorious inevitability of surprises and the discovery of the unknown. If you knew at the outset what you were going to discover and how you were going to do it, then what's the point? The more you learn about your subject, the more refined your questions will become, and you will learn things you knew nothing or very little about which will, in turn, lead you to new and even more refined and interesting questions and, hopefully, answers. Without surprises, serendipity, curious mistakes, wrong turns, and moments of "aha!" research would not be worth doing. Perhaps the most important trait for a doctoral student to have is curiosity and willingness to fail and try again. I know I would have had more fun, and probably produced a better dissertation, if I had these attitudes while in school. But unfortunately, for much of my dissertation process I was a mushy mass of insecurities and I ate spaghetti way too often.

18

It's Dissertation Time

This is it, the main event; the task for which you've been groomed. For the next who-knows-how-many years you will be researching and writing your way to the right to put three little letters and two periods after your name—Ph.D. This is also the most dangerous, difficult, and lonely period of the dissertation process. You have completed your proposal and done all the background research that entails. Your professors are confident that you can take the next step. And because you are one step closer to becoming a peer of your professors, a member of the Ph.D. "club," they are going to expect more independence on your part. Of course you will still get and need their feedback, but now is the time to show your stuff. Part of proving that you can research and write at a Ph.D. level is doing it largely on your own. Towards the end of the process, when you have draft chapters for review, your professors will provide more guidance, and they will provide the most guidance during the last push towards the defense. Yet, before that point, don't expect too much handholding. There are going to be many days when it is just you and the books or the laboratory.

Before getting to the specifics of writing the dissertation it is important to talk about three very important letters—ABD.

19

When You Can't or
Don't Want to go on

Many of those who begin doctoral programs never finish. Some drop out near the beginning, either before the coursework is completed or before the general exams. Those who make it through the coursework and exams but go no further are referred to as being All But Dissertation (ABD). There are no good estimates on how many ABDs there are, but the number is certainly quite large, perhaps as high as 50 percent of all students who make it through their general exams.

No matter how distasteful and upsetting it may be to leave a doctoral program before finishing, especially when so much time, energy, and money has been invested, there are extremely valid reasons for doing so. Money could be an issue. You might have lost interest in your research and find it torturous or your career goals might have shifted, making the Ph.D. seem less necessary and more of a bother than a help. Or, perhaps you were discovered by a Hollywood talent agent and asked to star in a major motion picture or the Prize Patrol knocked on your door during the Super Bowl to give you $10 million, and you decided, "hey I'm outta here."

Whatever are your positive reasons for leaving, just make sure that you weigh them fully against the potential negatives. Will you feel guilty for leaving because you think it is a sign of failure? Are you so close to getting your degree that leaving now would, under less stressful circumstances, seem a rash action? Has the stress of the situation blown the problems way out of proportion and would a short break help you regroup? There are many other reasons for and against swelling the ranks of the ABDs. The most important thing is that you consider the pros and cons fully and are comfortable with your decision. If you are, then you can leave your doctoral program with your head held high.

I came very close to becoming an ABD. Four months before I finished I was very pessimistic about my prospects for graduating. My topic, which had already changed twice, was growing tiresome. I found it hard to frame clear questions, much less come to clear answers. The opinions of the scholars who populated my field took precedence over my own. My opinion on how to frame and evaluate the issues would change in step with the book or article I was reading at the time. Lacking confidence in my own thought process, I sought refuge in the thoughts of others but never found what I was looking for. Worst of all my reason for getting a Ph.D. had vanished. I initially sought the degree because I wanted to be a professor. Slowly, I lost interest in that career. There were many reasons why. Although I enjoyed teaching, I didn't enjoy academic research or writing the type of scholarly pieces that would enable me to get tenure at a good university or college. I didn't want to spend my time testing hypotheses, constructing sound research methodologies, and coming to normative conclusions. And because I didn't want to do these things, I knew I wouldn't be very successful even if I tried. If you're not passionate about something as all-consuming as academic research, or any pursuit for that matter, then you'd best find another outlet for your energy and creativity. By the time I had finished my fifth year, I knew I would never be a professor, but I plowed on, believing that I had enough energy left to get the degree. Then, my energy level plummeted and my mood soured.

My sleep became erratic and depression affected my relationships with my wife, my family, and friends. The worst part was my relationship with myself. It is said that adversity introduces a man to himself. Well, I didn't like the person I had become. The indecision that marked my research and writing permeated my being. Although I knew I wanted my Ph.D., I was not at all confident that I was going to get it. Some days, dropping out seemed like the only, albeit worst alternative.

Interaction with my main professor only seemed to make things worse. Our relationship had become very difficult for both of us. He couldn't understand why I was having such a difficult time and must have found our discussions painful since he wanted to help but wasn't sure how. I felt he had lost confidence in me and I knew I was a pitiful sight. Despite this, it was a single conversation with this professor that helped me turn the corner. As I sat on the couch in his office he told me in a firm voice that he knew I was capable of getting a doctorate and that my research and questions were good enough to write an acceptable dissertation. He said I had to buckle down and finish a draft of the dissertation in four months or leave the program. Either way his main message was clear—stop torturing yourself and those around you and get on with your life.

Exactly four months later I handed in a complete draft. Three weeks after that I successfully defended my dissertation. Two weeks later I moved from Boston, with my wife, and began a new job in Washington, D.C. The turnaround was dramatic for all involved. I felt extremely relieved and couldn't stop smiling. Friends couldn't stop congratulating me. And my family was very proud, not so much because I was now a doctor, but because I hadn't given up so close to the end.

My wife reacted most dramatically. In the days after my defense the time we spent together seemed very strange to her. The only Eric she had ever known was "dissertation Eric." Now that the weight was off my shoulders, in her eyes I had become a new man virtually overnight. Two husbands for the price of one. Fortunately, she liked the second version even better than the first.

Having just read about my travails, you may be depressed or worried. If the process takes such a toll, is it really worth it? Shame on you for jumping to this conclusion. As a doctoral student you should know better than to generalize from one case study. My story is just one out of tens of thousands that are out there or have yet to be created. I know of many doctoral students whose experiences were not as traumatic as mine. And I do not regret my years or tears as a doctoral student. Amidst the pain, there were many moments of joy. Some of them even lasted for ten minutes. Seriously, during my doctorate I met and fell in love with the woman who became my wife, I made some friends, went to movies and plays, participated in athletic events, took classes with talented individuals, learned fascinating things from brilliant minds, and ate a ton of ice cream. So, take heart. Life is what you make of it. And, yes that even applies to weenie-headed doctoral students like you.

20

The Dreaded Question

One of the most difficult things you will confront in writing your dissertation is THE QUESTION. At times, it's as if friends and family have only one thing on their mind, namely, when are you going to be done? It's not THE QUESTION that's unnerving, but rather the frequency with which it's asked and the various forms it takes. During my years as a doctoral student, hundreds of people professed interest in my academic progress. For some, the interest was merely polite. "So, how much more time do you have left," they would inquire. After hearing my response, which varied depending on the content and tone of my last discussion with my advisors, the questioner usually moved the conversation in another direction.

But others liked to see me squirm. For one of my friends, finding out how many years I thought I had left wasn't enough for him. Adding that number to the time I had already spent in the doctoral program his expression quickly changed from one of mild concentration to deep concern. I sensed danger. "Is that normal," he asked. "Yes," I replied, although I had my doubts upon recalling the definition of normal appearing in *Webster's Third New International Dictionary*, which states, in part, that a normal being is one that is "free from intellectual defect."

Unsatisfied with my claim of normality, my friend asked, "don't you want to finish sooner," a variant of another oft-asked question, "can't you finish sooner?" I responded by pointing out the difficulties involved in getting a Ph.D., including the time required to come up with a researchable question, the long hours in the library, the frustrations involved in getting data, and the obstacles faced in trying to get your dissertation committee to agree that either you've done enough or that it would be cruel and unusual punishment to have you rewrite your dissertation for the Nth time. I also told him about the joy of learning that has no expiration date, the fun and excitement that keeps you researching and writing day after day, and the fact that good doctoral programs are in the business of providing pleasure, not pain. I felt justified, but he remained unconvinced. His parting comment was, "it's taking you that long even though you already had a masters in the same field before starting the doctoral program?"

THE QUESTION is easier to take when it comes from someone who doesn't know better. At a party, one of my distant cousins asked me when I was planning to graduate. When I told her my prediction her only response was, "I know why you stay in school, you just don't like to work." Since money, not education is what she values, her pronouncement was understandable. What is less understandable, however, are academics and Ph.D.'s who ask how long until you're done. They should know better. Fortunately many of them don't ask too often or at all.

The most difficult person to deal with, by far, is oneself. As the days melt into weeks, weeks months, and months into years you can't help but ask, "when will I be through?" This is especially true if financing your education is particularly difficult. This question, though, goes well beyond the simple passage of time and indebtedness. When doctoral students measure their progress, it is also in terms of analytical competence, subject mastery, and intellectual confidence. These are achievements that never come easily and are always part of a process that takes many years. The process never really ends.

One technique you might consider in dealing with THE QUESTION is lying. Tell your interrogator that you are on the verge of discovering a totally new compound. There are still years of work to do, but when it's over you'll be famous. If exaggerating is not your style, try underrating. Tell people you are in the midst of an epic battle with your mind and are not convinced you'll win. Mention the visions that come to you late at night and the hours you spend hitting the return key on your computer. Invite them to come to your house and sit with you in the darkness, wearing all black, while you mourn for western civilization. Whatever course you choose, the bigger the lie the more likely you'll get these people to move on to a different line of questioning.

21

Conference Mania

You can't be an academic without attending at least one conference a year. These gatherings of like-minded individuals are where you can share ideas and network. They can be a critical factor in determining the trajectory of your research and your life after graduation. Contacts made at conferences can be parlayed into jobs. And if you present a paper that is a big hit, you may even get people pursuing you and your talent.

Before you go to a conference you will need to do two things. First, get ready to eat and drink late into the night, while staying awake during hour after hour of talks, some of which can be quite stultifying. Conferences are as much social events as intellectual gatherings. Sometimes the best intellectual discourse takes place over a nice bowl of fettuccine alfredo and a glass of chardonnay. Second, you'll need to have a short and neat speech ready to describe who you are and why you are worthy of attention. As soon as you meet someone new at one of these conferences, the clock starts ticking. Each of you will do your best to use any cues you can to size up the person standing in front of you. In determining whether it is worthwhile to continue conversing with this person you will try to divine as quickly as possible whether the being before you is interesting and, better yet, can contribute anything to your rapid ascent into the ionosphere of intellectual achievement. That is why it is important to make a good first impression and to do so fast. Here are two examples, one of how to do it right and the other of how not to.

> **You:** Hello, my name is John Wiz and I'm working on solving one of the most vexing problems confronting academia today. Namely, why people

often fail to maximize utility in the face of a social landscape that is laden with opportunities for success. Once I discover why people are not truly rational actors, I will develop a theorem that, when applied by normal individuals, will lead them to turn around their less than optimal lives and become super-people, completely satisfied, confident, and financially secure. I expect my defense to be a blast. Once I'm through with my current work I will tackle homelessness.

The person you are talking to: Wow, what's your name again?

Or;

You: My name is Joanne Bland. I don't have a question yet. I'm not sure when I'll be through with my dissertation. This cabernet sauvignon tastes a bit fruity, what do you think?

The person you are talking to: Take a look at those hors d'oeuvres. Will you excuse me?

Of course, the most important thing at any academic conference is coffee. Hour after hour of talks, no matter how interesting, can really take it out of you. A strong cup of Java can save you from nodding off in front of some luminary in your field, who incidentally will probably never forget your face.

Another key attribute of conferences is the location. Of course your reason for attending is to learn, but still you're going to want to have some extracurricular fun. The rule of thumb is that for every two days of conference time, you have to take at least 3 hours off to sightsee and relax. This is always more enjoyable when the conference location offers excellent attractions. If you doubt this assumption, then why are so many conferences in exciting places? If the conference organizers wanted you to focus solely on the talks and official functions, then why don't they have their conferences at a dump of a hotel just off the interstate in the midst of an industrial landscape? Nobody would come, that's why. In the face of stiff competition from other conferences, each conference organizer tries to get the most desirable destination, to pull you in. A big chunk of every conference prospectus focuses on what you can do with your free time. Why, if not for the importance of the entertainment factor?

22

Footnoting Your Way to a Degree

Footnotes are one of the basic building blocks of academic arguments. They are the mortar that you use to piece together your very own tower of intellectual power. By citing those who came before you and upon whose shoulders you are standing, you can wrap yourself and your thoughts in the mantle of scholarship and signal to the reader that you are not only conversant in the language and theory of your field, but you can also use that knowledge in presenting your unique voice. Footnotes are also a great way to keep from being labeled a plagiarist by your peers for using the ideas and arguments of others without attribution and, thereby, giving the false appearance of original thought. The key is to know how and when to use footnotes to their best advantage.

The beginning doctoral student is likely to use footnotes liberally, but not excessively. You want to show your teachers that you are familiar with the literature, but don't want to overdo it. As time goes on, however, the pull of the footnote will grow stronger. Formerly innocuous phrases and thoughts, seemingly obvious conclusions and facts, will have to be referenced. This might be because some of your past work was impugned in some manner and you are going to compensate for this by adding more footnotes because you believe that there is a direct correlation between the number of footnotes and the depth of your scholarship. Alternatively, your footnotes could be reproducing because you really like the way they look at the bottom of the page. Either way, you must resist the impulse to justify your every utterance by footnoting another source. Take control of your life and your thoughts. Give credit where credit is due, but shamelessly and confidently grab the limelight and bask in the glory of your own mind and your own thoughts whenever you can. Think, man, think, and by thinking become a doctoral original, an academic supernova, a man whose mind will generate awe in other students and inspire imitation. Well, maybe that's overstating it a bit, but you get the idea.

"HELLO, HOTLINE? I HAVE A PROBLEM..."

23

Rotten Results

The Ph.D. process is an exploration into the unknown. You have a question but don't know the answer. On the way to getting an answer you will undoubtedly head down numerous intellectual dead-ends, perform experiments that fail, and find data that seems to contradict your pet theories. This is normal. If everything went smoothly what fun would that be? Okay, if that happened it would be freakin' fantastic, but don't hold your breath. Creating something new is a process of trial and error. Each wrong turn will move you that much closer to the place you want to be. "If at first you don't succeed, try, try again" is not only a hackneyed cliche, it is excellent advice for anyone, especially a doctoral student who is trying to chart new territory.

Still, even the most optimistic among us might get a bit frustrated when things don't work out as planned. Just imagine how you would feel if you found that a large amount of experimental data you had painstakingly collected was junk. I know how one person reacted. He had been doing very complicated genetic test in the laboratory for a little over a year, only to discover that one of the key instruments was calibrated incorrectly. Mounds of data became worthless. To his credit, after he stopped crying and cursing, he started anew and finally finished his dissertation, about a year later than originally anticipated.

24

Go Jump

There is a fundamental difference between the hard sciences and the soft or social sciences. In the hard sciences, like physics and chemistry, practitioners spend a lot of time developing or, more accurately, revealing laws that are actually laws. They tell you how the world or some small part of it operates, or how it will operate given certain inputs, and they do a very good job of that. For example, any good physicist will tell you that there is no such thing as a perpetual motion machine, and that you can't make something out of nothing. Similarly, engineers have some pretty good laws or rules they rely on to predict the future, given certain inputs. That is why we usually feel comfortable driving over bridges. We have confidence that the engineers have applied the rules of their profession in determining how strong the bridge has to be in order not to collapse when a min-van filled with four screaming kids jumping up and down drives over it.

The soft sciences, like political science and sociology, on the other hand, don't have nearly as many laws of behavior, and even when they are present, they are not nearly as capable of predicting the future as the laws applied by their colleagues in the hard sciences. Although soft scientists do their best to produce predictive laws of cause and effect, they always have to deal with those nasty variables, human nature and the inherent unpredictability of human interactions. And there's the rub. Ask a political scientist to tell you why a certain piece of legislation got passed and yet failed to produce good results during the implementation phase, and you can usually count on a compelling analysis of what happened and why. However, if you ask the same person to tell you how you should structure a new law and set up the implementation process so that the law's application will be efficient and effective and achieve the stated goals, she will undoubtedly give you an answer, but if she gave you, say 80 percent odds that following her advice would achieve the exact results you want, then you ought to find a more honest social scientist. This is not to imply that the research done by soft scientists is useless. On the contrary, it is often very useful and has provided society with valuable insights into a whole range of behaviors and interactions, and as well has contributed mightily to positive societal change. But, the soft sciences, no matter how they try, will never be like the hard sciences, and thank goodness for that. Just imagine how many soft scientists would be unemployed if, say, the political process were reduced to clear and unwavering operational and behavioral rules that could be gleaned from a basic book on political science that anybody could pick up at the local bookstore. There would then be no need for yet another dissertation or book on the strengths and weaknesses of the policy process and how that process should be changed. Then again, if the ultimate laws of policymaking were, indeed, knowable, then we could all stop complaining about the policy-making process and, instead, spend our time doing important stuff, like watching television.

But, if you are a social scientist, you're in luck. There will always be more room for another dissertation, another crack at furthering our understanding of human processes and interactions. Be prepared, however, for at some point during your dissertation, your professor is going to ask you make the so-called "normative leap," which is moving from merely describing the facts of a situation or problem to making recommendations on what ought to be done to improve the situation or resolve the problem. The conversation might go something like this.

> **Professor:** You're going to have to go beyond telling me every detail of what happened during the development and implementation of the National Environmental Policy Act and tell me how you think the Act should be changed to ensure that more wildlife species are not obliterated by expanding development pressures.

> **You:** Really? I thought that if I wrote long enough and submitted numerous dissertation drafts, we'd eventually call it a day and you'd give me my doctorate. I hadn't fully comprehended the "original thought" aspect of the degree.

"HE'LL BE ALL RIGHT. HE'S ABOUT TO MAKE HIS 'NORMATIVE LEAP.'"

Professor: You are a zit on the rump of academia. Nevertheless, we let you into this institution and we are not going to kick you out until we have sucked as much money as possible from you and made you go through the torturous, mind-bending process of actually writing a dissertation.

You: If that's the way you feel about it, all right. What do I have to do?

Professor: You have to take the normative leap. You have to summon up the courage to look at the story you have told, to review what happened and why, and then tell your committee how the Act needs to be changed to achieve the policy goals you feel are most integral to the Act's existence. Just do it. Take the normative leap, man!

You: About how far do I have to jump?

Professor: Get out of here this instant, you miserable lump of sod.

If you've reached this part of the doctoral program, you can do one of two things. You can tell your committee to go jump, or you can make up something that sounds like normative analysis and might actually fool your committee into awarding you the degree. Of course, there is a third option; namely, taking the normative leap and having confidence you won't land on your face. Even if you do land on your face, don't worry, you'll have plenty of company. It's a law of nature that you can't go through a doctoral program without falling on your face at least twice. The important thing is, to get up, wipe yourself off, and walk up to the ledge again and again until you can make the normative leap.

25

Are You Jungian, Freudian, or just Pissed Off?

Each discipline has its own language that serves to identify the initiated and exclude others. The proper term for this verbiage is jargon. A little jargon here, a little jargon there, add a few obscure journals and a bit of money, and soon you have a new department. As a doctoral student you must not be scared of jargon. Ease into the lingo slowly. And remember jargon is your friend.

Listening to the masters of minutiae use jargon to express themselves can be a surreal experience. Consider the following.

> The site has not been fully remediated. Therefore the hazard quotient of entering the restrictive perimeter is exceedingly high. We did a titration of the effluent coming from the site and are planning to do some spectrographic and chromatographic analysis of the samples. We have identified the principally responsible party and have determined that, under the applicable statutory regime, he is jointly and severally liable for punitive damages, which could be meted out by a wise judge through the use of her adjudicative powers.

There are two possible translations of this:

> 1—This place is full of hazardous waste, and man, I wouldn't go in there if you paid me. We're using ridiculously expensive machines to figure out what this crap is. Oh yeah, we know who did it. We're gonna get him. He

did it and it's a no-brainer for the judge. This guy is going to pay through the nose.

2—How did such a little kid produce so much crap? It's the poop from hell and it's dangerous in here. I think that it was the pureed prunes that did it, but to be really sure I need to look a bit closer. What do you mean, "did he do it," he's the only kid we've got and just look at the diaper—yeech! He's your son, you change him.

The truly gifted among us are those who can speak in acronyms.

"Hello Bob, are you the AA for the FDIC, the DOL, or the USFWS, and did you send me that FYEO report discussing the ANPR that will appear in the FR? By the way, I'm interested in responding to the RFP I saw in CBD. Do you have any suggestions for my proposed SOW, and does it have to include a methodology for the CBA I plan to do on the entire REGNEG process? What's that you say, I'm SOL because the POTUS zeroed out the program. Man, he's a SOB.[1]

There is an unsubstantiated story that a professor at MIT became so proficient in the use of acronyms that he discarded all nouns, verbs, adverbs, gerunds, past participles, present pluperfects, adjectives, and conjunctions. All he had left were acronyms, which he disgorged in spasmodic spurts of communication.

The problem with jargon is that as your discipline becomes more specialized there are fewer and fewer people with which you can have an intelligible conversation. If you get too carried away the only person you'll be able to speak with is yourself.

---

1.   The acronyms stand for: AA—Assistant Administrator; FDIC—Federal Deposit Insurance Corporation; DOL—Department of Labor; USFWS—United States Fish and Wildlife Service; FYEO—for your eyes only; ANPR—advanced notice of proposed rulemaking; FR—Federal Register; RFP—request for proposal; CBD—Commerce Business Daily; SOW—statement of work; CBA—cost-benefit analysis; REGNEG—regulatory negotiation; SOL—shit out of luck; POTUS—President of the United States; and SOB—if you don't know what this stands for you have led too sheltered of a life.

26

The Long and Winding Road or the Tunnel of Love

Now that you are well into your dissertation research you have probably come to the central question posed by doctoral students the world over, which is, what the hell am I doing here? There is no single answer. You'll have to work through your own history, personality, neuroses, personal predilections, quirks, and idiosyncrasies to determine how to answer this question. You may even have to hire a whole army of psychiatrists to answer this one.

Some of you, of course, may never face this question. You may be one of those extremely well-adjusted, brilliant doctoral students who studies and writes volumes by the day, reads novels for fun at night, has mastery of the relevant literature, doesn't panic during tests, attends departmental seminars and asks provocative questions, loves to develop working and null hypotheses, gets excited by causal connections and footnotes, always answers every idea presented to him/her with a thoughtful "that's interesting," works-out on a regular basis, maintains a lively, written correspondence with peers and friends, finds the Dewey-decimal system engrossing, and never gets down on themselves.

Congratulations! You are a rare individual. Just try to keep your existence to yourself, because you're getting the rest of the average, run-of-the-mill, depressed, struggling doctoral students down. Look at them, for God's sakes. They go to the library every day, wearing drab clothes, and take notes endlessly as a way of putting off actually writing and saying something original. They have platinum copy cards. The last time they read for enjoyment was in high school and that wasn't really much fun anyway. They have plenty of peers, but don't tend to associate with them. Friends, are you kidding? When presented with a new idea, they flee, for they don't need more ideas, they want answers. To them relevant literature means everything written by the professors on their committee; they don't have time for much else. Tests make them plotz. The thought of asking a question at a seminar is terrifying. Their muscles, with the exception of those required to turn pages and copy, are atrophied.

Okay, so I'm exaggerating a bit. Actually, most doctoral students fall into the middle of these extremes. That's to be expected. As I said earlier, getting Ph.D. is hard work and somebody has got to do it. And that somebody is you.

27

So, You Want to be a Professor

Many people pursue doctoral degrees because they want to teach at a college or university. Teaching is a noble profession and a great professor can have an enormously positive impact on your education and your life. Being a good professor, however, is not easy. Being an expert in your field, with a deep knowledge of the literature and a highly analytical mind, is only part of what is necessary. You also need to be able to translate your enthusiasm and intellectual curiosity to your students. And, most of all, you have to love being a professor, including the give-and-take and the debate inside and out of the classroom, and the desire to help students learn and become inspired by what they learn. To see if you have what it takes to be a good, or perhaps even a great professor, try your hand at teaching before you get your degree.

Most doctoral students get a taste of teaching through being a TA. If you are lucky, you can get beyond merely grading papers, to running labs and holding office hours to answer questions from students. When you get before a class for the first time, you'll be nervous. That's normal. Here is an example of what to expect.

You: Hello class, my name is John. I'll be the TA for this class.

Student 1: Do you have a last name, Johnny boy?

You: Yes, it's Smythe, s-m-y-t-h-e, but you can call me John. No need for formality.

Student 1: That's an odd spelling. Are you an odd fellow?

You: Let's get on with the class, shall we. Today, I want to discuss what I expect you to get out of these labs.

Student 2: You're a doctoral student, right? What year are you?

You: First year.

Student 2: Let's see, that makes you first semester, first year. You haven't even learned anything yet. I would have thought we'd have gotten at least a fourth or fifth year doctoral student.

You: I assure you I know my material and can certainly run this lab. Why don't you give me chance?

Student 3: How about we give you two problems to solve. If you get them both of them right, you can stay.

You: Okay, that's enough, you pathetic bunch of whiners. I didn't fight my way through four years of college and two years of graduate school, to take crap from peons such as you. I might not know much more than you do, but I do have control over your lab grade, which, as I was going to tell you, constitutes 25 percent of your course grade. So, the next time you want to treat me with disrespect, remember that I control a little part of your future. Any questions?

Students in unison: No, Mr. Smythe.

Whether you're taking classes or are a TA, pay close attention to your professors. Note their teaching style. Keep a list of good traits and bad traits. That way you will be able to develop your own sense of what it takes to be a great professor, as well as what it takes to fail miserably. To get you started, here are some candidates for inclusion on your list.

Good Traits

Knows the theoretical and applied literature in the field

Is a clear, forceful, and animated speaker

Is well organized

Shows up to class on time

Treats students with respect

Returns problem sets, papers, and tests quickly

Offers comments on your work that are encouraging and will help you learn how to improve your work

Grades fairly

Encourages debate and courteous disagreement

Loves mentoring students, answering their questions, and spending time with them outside of class, during office hours and department functions

Has good connections with others in the field and an understanding of what issues are on the cutting edge

Bad Traits

Knows everything about one theory and is not interested in applying it

Speaks with mouth half open, usually with his back to the class

Sometimes falls asleep or goes into a trance-like state in mid-sentence

Believes, with all his being, in personal chaos theory

Shows up to class after it is over

Views students as temporary annoyances that have to be endured

Returns problem sets, papers, and tests 30 to 60 days from receipt

His favorite comment on student work is, "they don't pay me enough to read this drivel"

Relies on spurious and confounding variables to establish grade (For example, if you have more than twelve letters in your name, you get a demerit of 10 points out of 100. And if give an answer on an essay question that is so good that he doubts he could have penned a better one himself, you're docked 20 points.)

Cuts students off if they disagree with him and prefers that they all just keep their thoughts to themselves

Runs out of class to avoid casual interactions with students

Instead of keeping office hours, keeps office minutes

Avoids department functions like the plague

Does not care about your future, except to ensure that it doesn't involve him

After being exposed to teaching, if you aren't enthusiastic about becoming a professor and/or you are fairly sure you wouldn't be a good one anyway, I've got some friendly advice. Don't become a professor who has to teach. Go to your strengths and avoid forcing others to deal with your weaknesses. Do something else with your life and save countless students pain and anguish!

28

Relax, You'll Live Longer

One of the most difficult things to do while writing a dissertation is relax. I don't mean just stop working and do something fun like go to a movie or read for pleasure. I mean really relax to the point where you feel calm and don't even think about your dissertation at all. An inability to relax is certainly understandable. Writing a dissertation is one of the most focused experiences you will ever have. It is as engrossing and all encompassing as it can be frustrating. But, if you don't relax your dissertation prose will be as tight and twisted as that knot in your neck.

During my dissertation I found it very hard to relax. I became so wrapped up in my work that I would talk incessantly about my hypotheses, my case studies, and my lack of progress in coming to conclusions. I became a virtual if-then, yeah-but machine, sputtering about causal connections that I couldn't quite find, and the anguish of it all. It got so bad that my wife made me promise that I would leave all my thoughts about the dissertation at the door to our bedroom. That most private of places was to be our refuge from school and our place to reconnect. For a week I kept my word. Then, on the eighth night I stood in the doorframe. My wife, already in bed, looked up at me. We stared for a while. I could stand it no longer. I started talking about my dissertation and the horrible day I'd had. She yelled, "you're not supposed to talk about that in our bedroom." But I had her. I wasn't actually in the bedroom, I said, just at the threshold. She quietly got up and shut the door in my face.

OCCASIONALLY YOU NEED TO CRAWL OUT FROM UNDER THE PRESSURE OF YOUR DISSERTATION.

One thing you can do to relax is to occasionally go out with people who aren't in your program. Better yet, spend some quality time away from people who have or want to have a Ph.D. You know what happens when you're in the company of other Ph.D. students. Inevitably the topic of conversation turns to the doctoral process. Before you know it, you're trading stories while your non-Ph.D. bound friends suffer in silence, jabbing at their Kung Pao chicken. And whatever you do don't hang out with more than two other people with whom you share the same main professor. This is a recipe for disaster. No sooner will you exchange pleasantries, than you'll launch into an in-depth bull session about the strengths, weaknesses, and general sadistic tendencies of your professor. You'll recount meetings with that professor or comments she made and imbue them with mystical, almost spiritual meaning as you try to divine the essence of the interaction. You'll discuss the professor's quirks and peculiarities with a glee that borders on fanaticism. He smiled at me upon saying I would be out of here in just two years. What the hell did that mean? Was he serious? Was he jesting? Am I gonna spend the rest of my life chained to this &^%$#*@ computer?

Whatever you do, stay away from the doctoral students who have been in your program too long. Conversations with them could lead to permanent psychological scarring. Take, for example, the guy on the 10-year plan. He has compiled a bibliography that weighs five pounds, which he has with him at all times. He mumbles, but can, when moved, quote passages from the classics in the field at will. He has been a TA for every course in the department, twice. His coffee cup has growth rings. He had planned to be done in four. He views his main professor as a godlike figure with powers over life and death. The other committee members are the apostles. His shoulders are rounded from hunching over books. He has a permanent carrel in the school library. All the librarians know him by name. He has no need for punctuation or anti-perspirant. He rides an old broken down bike, and wears a beret and tweed jackets with jeans. He is the ghost of a doctoral student's future, and the best argument for going to law school.

29

Your Significant Other

You're going to need all the support you can get during the doctoral process. The person you'll lean on most heavily is your significant other, whether that is your lover, wife, husband, partner, or alien being. Be very, very nice to this person because when you stumble you want to make sure someone is there to help you up, and when you succeed you'll want to share the joy.

My significant other was my wife, Jennifer. She went well beyond the call of duty in the last three years of my dissertation process. During most of that time we were not even married, which makes her devotion and understanding all the more remarkable.

Jennifer added loving perspective when I lost it. Each morning she left for work and wished me luck as I slunk off to the back room in our apartment where the computer was. When she returned I would shuffle to the door, hug her, and proclaim in a pitiful voice, "I wrote two sentences today." Whereupon Jennifer looked me in the eye, shook my shoulders and responded, "what is your problem? This dissertation is just a Big #$%*&@! Paper, not *War and Peace*. Write something, anything, I don't care what, just write. And why haven't you made me dinner?"

Jennifer was also good at faking interest. Each night I would inquire, "could I ask you question about my dissertation?" Then I would recount one of my arguments and ask if it made any sense. Jennifer usually said it sounds good to me, to which I responded by methodically picking apart the argument I had just laid out. I was my own worst enemy. Realizing she couldn't win, Jennifer usually rolled over and went to sleep.

Your significant other can be helpful in other ways. For example, Jennifer would occasionally come into my "dissertation room" and jump up and down on my piles of paper. The first time I asked what she was doing, she said "I'm trying to condense all this stuff down into chapters for you." It didn't work, but she seemed to have a good time.

No matter how engrossed or obsessed you become about your dissertation, you cannot ignore those around you, especially your significant other. You must, on a regular basis, take time out to forget about your dissertation or the latest book on the newest theory, and instead focus on those who really count. Your Ph.D. is a piece of paper, albeit an important one, but the people who surround you are your life and without them you might get pretty lonely when it's just you and your diploma hanging out on a Saturday night. So, take breaks, give back the support you're receiving and, in the immortal words of my sister, "stop sniveling."

30

A Word to the Significant Others

Yours is a particularly tough job. You will vicariously experience the ups and downs of the dissertation process. You will hear the stories about the professors, the classes, the exams, the fellow students, and that damn question. You will undoubtedly be asked to read and re-read draft after draft of the dissertation, listen to new ideas, and suffer through the tough times that every Ph.D. student encounters.

For all this sacrifice you will receive no pay. People who know little or nothing about the Ph.D. process will not understand what you're going through. Even those who are familiar with the process might be less than sympathetic.

Whatever your experience as the significant other, if this doctoral student is the one for you, hang in there. The dissertation process will end one way or another. For every relationship that weathers the process, probably just as many don't. From my observations, those that do survive become stronger because of the difficulties they endured.

When times get tough, here are some tips that might help you cope better:

Zone out

During one particularly trying stretch I called my wife at least once a day just to talk about the dissertation and the difficulties I was having. Usually, she would listen politely and comment sporadically. Sometimes she was very silent. About one year after I completed my dissertation, I found out what those silences meant. Jennifer had fallen asleep on the phone. My problems had become so repetitive that they put her to sleep like a nightmarish lullaby. She knew how to protect herself.

Get out of the house

When things get particularly difficult, leave, if only for a while and do something you enjoy. Time away can be invigorating and remind you why you love this person who is going through their Ph.D. My wife's favorite escape was to her parent's house, just a forty-minute drive from where we lived. There she would recuperate and have a good meal. Her folks, in turn, would inquire, as nicely as possible, as to why she was putting up with this crap. To which she would respond, it'll pass. Actually, her parents were very supportive of her and me, but they did wonder why I was in such a state and urged me to get the dissertation over with, and fast. Far from annoying me, Jennifer's parents' comments provided one more reason why I needed to finish.

Give advice when asked, but don't expect too much

Doctoral students often ask for advice about their dissertation. How does this hypothesis sound? Is this a plausible argument? Does this make sense? Say what you feel, but don't be slighted if your advice goes unheeded. Doctoral students can get so wrapped up in their work that they fail to take good advice when it is offered. During the latter part of my dissertation, my professors and fellow students told me many things that I had already heard from Jennifer. Yet, hearing the comments from an outside source seemed to have a greater impact.

Time-out

In order to maintain balance in your life and the life of the person getting their doctorate, it is a good idea to plan days, weekends, or longer if you like, to leave the dissertation behind. This need to truly relax was covered earlier, but it is so important that it deserves mention again. Go on a hike, visit a bed & breakfast in a picturesque town, watch a parade, take a drive in the country, have a picnic, or go to a concert or play. Before doing any of this, however, agree that discussion or thoughts about the dissertation are out of bounds. It'll clear your mind and give you energy you can use to attack the research and writing when you return.

31

Friends and Family

Friends are an integral part of the fabric of life. They provide support when you're down and camaraderie when you're on a more even keel. Life without good friends is inconceivable. They are a resource that must be treasured. As with any critical resource, it is important that you conserve them as best you can. This doesn't mean you should avoid leaning on your friends when times get tough. That is, after all, the truest test of a good friend. But friends, like your significant other, can only take so much. Share both the good and the bad and try to keep it weighted towards good. This will nourish the relationship and make it that much more likely that your friends will be there when things aren't going your way. If you are a miserable, shriveled-up doctoral student you might still have friends, but they'll be difficult to find.

Whether or not you have a significant other or friends, you probably have family. Be nice to them. They can be another source of support and encouragement. It's in their best interest to be there for you. If you fail, your relatives look bad. And since they are genetically related to you, your failure will lead to questions about the quality of your family's part of the gene pool. Nobody wants that, especially if any of your relatives fear that they are already a bit too close to the shallow end of the gene pool!

Before I met Jennifer, my family members were the first ones I turned to when I needed to talk. A typical call to my folks might be as follows:

Me: Hello mom, it's me. I'm falling apart. My research stinks and I haven't written a word today. Nobody likes me. I ate macaroni and cheese for dinner, again. How are you?

Mom: I knew I should have breast fed you. Maybe Uncle Bob pulling your arm out if its socket, repeatedly, is the problem. Macaroni and cheese doesn't help either. You should be eating vegetables and chicken, but stay away from the butter. Here, speak to your father.

Dad: Son. Are you whining again? You're driving your mom and me nuts. Can't you just buck up and take it like a man? Every time you call, your mom spends the rest of the night talking about your eating habits. I can't take it anymore. Stop eating that damn macaroni and cheese and finish your doctorate.

Me: Thanks, dad. I love you man.

My sister wasn't much better.

Me: Hello sis. I'm feeling kind of down right now. It's like I have writer's block. I can't get any coherent thoughts on paper (sob, sob). I just stare at the computer screen. I don't know what I'm going to do.

Sister: I told mom and dad that you were no good. They always paid more attention to you than me and see how you turned out. You're just a pile of barely differentiated protoplasm that is confused, alone, miserable, and scared. Oh, by the way, do you want to go in on a present for the folks' anniversary?

Me: I've got to go, my macaroni and cheese is getting cold.

My parent's greatest fear was that I would drop out of the Ph.D. program, move home, grow a beard, listen to Gregorian chants, become an extreme vegetarian, rarely get out of bed, read beat literature, write poetry, howl at the moon, hear voices emanating from light fixtures, communicate with aliens, claim that Oswald didn't act alone, believe that Esperanto is the language that could unify the world, fear the Trilateral Commission, collect belly-button lint, argue that professional wrestling is real, and watch daytime talk shows. They shouldn't have worried. I don't like poetry.

Actually, my parents and sister went well beyond the call of familial duty. They were there whenever I called and were always willing to listen and offer support and advice. They also believed in being truthful. Instead of "yessing" me to death, my family told me when they disagreed with my perceptions of a situation and they told when I was acting like a two-year old. It is no exaggeration to say that without my family and the support they gave, I wouldn't have finished my degree. Treasure your family and they will be there not only in the good times, but, more importantly, when everything seems to be going wrong.

32

The Secretary is all Powerful

Outside of your professor's office sits the secretary, a supremely powerful being. She controls the most important of all resources—access. In her hands you'll find the book. And on the pages of the book are the times that the professor has deigned to actually interact with the unwashed masses of students who seek his wisdom. It is your fervent hope to have your name inscribed in the book, as are the names of the doctoral students from the days of yore. This will only happen if you get along with the secretary. Whatever you do, don't piss her off.

Brown-nosing is a delicate art, especially when dealing with secretaries. They've seen your kind before. They know what you want and they are fully aware of their ability to make you absolutely miserable. One strategy is to ask them about their life.

> **You:** How are you doing?
>
> **Secretary:** Fine.
>
> **You:** Are you feeling okay today?
>
> **Secretary:** Yes.
>
> **You:** How are your kids doing?
>
> **Secretary:** Fine.
>
> **You:** Is your husband doing okay?

Secretary: Yes.

You: Can I get fifteen minutes of professor Schnabel's time with the next two lunar cycles?

Secretary: You're pathetic.

Another approach is to buy them things.

You: Even though it's not Secretary's Day, I decided to honor your existence with this lovely bouquet of flowers. I grew them myself from seed.

Secretary: Thank you.

You: And that's not all. I know you like chocolate so I got you a sampler—one of everything they make. It cost a lot, but I think you're worth it. What's a little more debt when you're already in the hole for $40,000?

Secretary: You didn't get one of those cherry-filled ones? I hate them.

You: Do you think I could get some time with HIM next week?

Secretary: Ha! You gotta do better than that buddy. Last year one of your peers gave me an all-expenses paid weekend at a bed and breakfast in Vermont. I managed to squeeze him in a couple of months later.

Begging is another tactic.

You: Could I just have a little time with the professor? I'm a worthless piece of pond scum and I haven't had an original thought for three years. I don't even know why they accepted me, but I'm never gonna graduate without her help. You don't understand, my parents won't let me come home until I have a Ph.D.

Secretary: You're really pathetic. While you're down there on the floor, could you check under the desk for dust balls?

Perhaps the best approach of all is empathy.

You: It must be hard working for him. He's so demanding.

Secretary: You're so right. He relies on me to do everything. Type his letters, make his plane reservations, return calls, order books, call-in his prescriptions, coordinate the pickup of his kids, and tell his wife he loves her. He thinks I have no life.

You: That's horrible. You shouldn't let him use you like that. It's not fair.

Secretary: You wanted some time with him, right. How about this afternoon from 12-1? I'll just cancel his lunch appointment. He'll never know because I made it for him in the first place. He eats too much anyway.

You: You're the greatest.

33

Seeing Red

One of the things you're paying for at graduate school is feedback on your work from professors. A good professor will review draft dissertation chapters, see their strengths and weaknesses, and then provide comments which help you take the next step towards completion. The only problem with this process is that it can be painful.

This is especially true in the early stages of the dissertation. That is when you're testing out ideas and playing with the literature to see how it applies to your situation. You'll type up a draft chapter and print it out. It'll look good. So clean, so neat, and dotted with footnotes and carefully crafted sentences and/or equations. It's your creation and you're proud of it. You'll deliver it to your professor and then wait.

Days, weeks, or months later you'll get a call from your professor's secretary, the gatekeeper. "The time has come, it is ready," she'll say in a reverential tone. When you pick it up, do not look at it in the company of other people. Take it into the hall or a nearby bathroom or, better yet, an empty field. This is because when you see what has happened to the draft you put all that time and energy into, you might do something you wouldn't want other people to see, like cry.

What was neat and clean is now covered with red. Your professor has put your draft through his intellectual slicer and dicer and it's a bloody mess. What's worse, the chicken scrawl may be so bad that you can't read it. Don't despair. The comments are a good sign that your professor values your work and is willing to take the time to show you how it could be improved. If he didn't care, you would probably get few or no comments. Then again, maybe your professor really doesn't like you or your work at all. In that case, it is probably time to find a new professor.

34

Reaching out for Help

Many doctoral students go through periods of doubt and depression, sometimes serious, especially during the dissertation writing process. Fortunately, there are people you can turn to. Fellow students are one of the best sources of support. They are having similar experiences and would welcome the opportunity to talk to someone who understands. Thoughtful and concerned professors can also be a great source of support. A simple vote of confidence, coming from someone on your committee can boost your ego, enabling you to take the next steps. Similarly, don't overlook other staff within your department or the larger school. These people have seen doctoral students come and go. There is hardly a story they have not heard or a situation they have not seen. They, like your professors, might be able to offer some perspective on your situation. This is particularly important because perspective is one of the first casualties of the depressed mind.

There is another source of support that is often kept "hush-hush," but nevertheless is relied upon by more students and professors than you might think. This is professional help in the form of psychiatric or psychological therapy. Our society's taboo about reaching out in this manner is well known. But if you view mental health professionals as individuals whose training enables them to listen and help clarify your thoughts and emotions, such professional help is as an acceptable and often very positive option for the person seeking answers or at least more understanding. I know this first hand. On and off during the latter part of my doctoral program I saw a psychologist at school. I felt I needed someone totally detached from my life to talk to about how I was handling my dissertation. She didn't solve any of my problems, but I did find it helpful to talk to her.

If you find yourself needing some help dealing with your dissertation, reach out to those around you. And remember this is nothing to be ashamed of. It is an essential part of the human experience. You're definitely not alone.

35

The Home Stretch

At some point you'll decide, either on your own or with the prodding of your professor, that enough's enough. It's time to fish or cut bait, cook or get out of the kitchen, put up or shut up, roll the die and simply finish your dissertation or move on. One of the professors on my committee said to me early on that I better like my dissertation topic because by the end you're going to be sick of it. He was right. The key is to finish before you wretch or want to throw your computer off the nearest cliff.

Now is when your committee, which most likely has been a somewhat distant reality as you toiled in the stacks, comes back into view. You'll hand in chapter drafts and get comments back. Oftentimes, these comments will be quite helpful, urging you to refine your argument, tighten the text, or read a specific paper or book for some help in resolving a theoretical difficulty. Other times, the comments may not be so helpful, like "who let you into this program anyway," "a lowly masters student could have done this," or, (with apologies to Truman Capote) "this isn't research, it's typing."

You'll write, re-write, justify, gesticulate, copy, plead, laugh, cry, and pray to the gods of academia. Slowly, the dissertation will come together. Out of this mass of nouns, verbs, adjectives, and punctuation will appear cohesive paragraphs and chapters. Topic sentences will guide the way to clear hypotheses and conclusions. Causal connections will leap off the page. Computer programs will provide usable data. Your equations will comply with the laws of physics. There will be exhilarating moments when you solve a particularly thorny problem, or "chestnut" as some old-school academicians like to call them. Finally, the end is in sight. Then again, none of these things might happen. In that case, you're screwed.

36

The Best Defense is a Good Offense

There are two basic theories on the dissertation defense. To some it is a battle, the outcome of which is uncertain until the very end of the engagement. The specter of failing is very real, including the possibility of failing with no appeal. To others, the defense is a time to let a student who has written an acceptable dissertation show their stuff. In this case, the imagery is not of battle, and the outcome is clear going in. The student will pass, but not without having to face hard questions. And if the committee thinks that there is more work to be done, the dissertation is provisionally passed, contingent upon the student completing the final repairs within a reasonable period of time.

I cannot think of any reason to advocate the first theory. After years of work, the outcome should not hinge on a single event that lasts a couple of hours. Any properly functioning committee should know exactly how good the dissertation is and what the student knows. If, for some reason, a student who has written an adequate dissertation does a poor job defending himself because of nerves, lack of sleep, or whatever, that is not a good enough reason for her to fail. If, on the other hand, the student's defense is a shambles because the underlying dissertation is not good, then it is not the student's fault, but the committee's for letting the defense proceed. One of the committee's most important jobs is to decide when the student is ready and the only way to know this is by judging the quality of the dissertation itself. If the dissertation doesn't cut it, send the student back to the drawing board, don't draw and quarter him.

I've heard stories of doctoral students writing a good dissertation, falling apart during the defense, and still passing, though not without having to do some additional work. A doctoral student I know had a much worse experience. He was required to give a public lecture on his research, which was attended by his committee members and fellow students and friends. From the outset his professors peppered him with questions. After the lecture, his committee went into private session during which time they continued to attack the student's research and conclusions. Finally, one of his professors announced that the dissertation was a piece of junk and that to properly fix it would require the student to start again from the beginning with new questions and a better approach. The other committee members were not much more positive. Nevertheless, perhaps realizing that if their evaluation of his research were accurate, they deserved part of the blame, the committee grudgingly passed the student on the condition that he would do extensive work to improve the dissertation.

Recounting this story makes my blood boil. If the dissertation and the approach it was based on were that bad, the committee should have brought this to the student's attention much earlier. Instead, they failed in their jobs as mentors/advisors and left the student out to dry. Much to the student's credit, he went on to do the additional work, get his degree, landed a professorship and, last I heard, was publishing some high quality journal articles in his field. I doubt his committee members are on his holiday mailing list.

My situation was quite different. Unlike the defense described above, where the student presents a paper or answers questions in front of an audience, in my department it was solely a private affair, just you and your committee. As I waited outside my professor's office, I could hear my committee members laughing uproariously through the closed door. Unfortunately, or fortunately, I couldn't make out what they were laughing about. I started to get numb. I wanted to barge through the door and scream, "what are you laughing at? This is my life you're toying with!"

But there I sat in my suit and tie. The door opened and I was ushered in. My advisor started to speak. "On behalf of the committee,…" In my mind I thought, "no! no! Anything but on the 'behalf of the committee.' That's the kiss of death." He continued. "I would like you to know that we read your dissertation…" "Say it, say it," I silently screamed, "you think it's a piece of crap. Well, I think this whole process is a sham." I drifted back in time to hear him finish. "And we think you did a good job. You pass." I caught my breath. "What do you mean I pass?" I said. You were laughing just a minute ago. Is this a cruel joke? You would crush a young man's dreams like that? You mean you liked it? You really liked it? Okay, group hug."

Actually, I wasn't stunned by the outcome, but the swiftness of the delivery. I knew my professor. He subscribes to the second theory of the defense. He would not have let me into that room if he and the entire committee didn't think I had written an adequate dissertation. I hadn't expected, however, to be told I'd passed right away. The next sentence from my professor's mouth set the tone for the rest of the defense. He asked me why I was wearing a tie. I quickly took it off and asked him if he had anything to drink. "I thought you were going to bring that," was his response. They asked me a series of questions about my dissertation and, despite the relief I felt, my answers left a lot to be desired. Perhaps, I should have gone into writing after all.

So, how should you prepare for this final ritual in the dissertation process? There are different theories on this as well. I know of one guy who got drunk the night before and passed with flying colors. I do not recommend this. Many people will just study by themselves, reading their dissertation over and over again, and revisiting the relevant literature. Some convene study groups, where other doctoral students, friends, or relatives pepper the defender-to-be with questions. Others, still, do nothing or take a trip to clear the mind. They figure that, after all these years they're as ready as they will ever be, come what may. One tactic I have never heard of being used, but which might be very effective, is bringing your mother into the defense. Can you imagine a committee flunking you with mom in the room? After all, they have moms too. The most important thing is to pick the path that you find most comfortable. There is no wrong way to prepare for this test. Have faith in yourself and the process. Everything will probably work out fine.

As for how to comport yourself during the defense, here is a short list of do's and a longer list of don'ts:

Do:

Wear clothes (nudity will most likely distract your professors and detract from the dignity of the occasion)

Smile frequently, but not obsequiously

Reference at least one work published by each of the professors in the room

Respond to every third question posed with, "that's an interesting question"

Speak in complete sentences

Breath

Blink

Sit up straight

Bring something to drink (preferably alcoholic)

Think before answering

Don't:

Curl up in the fetal position (it would raise questions that you'd rather not answer)

Pray

Laugh uncontrollably

Beg for mercy

Request a second opinion

Offer to do anything

Ask if this will be multiple choice

Commend your committee on their smashing attire

Parade around the room, singing any of the following songs:

> "I won't grow up…"

> "I want you to want me, I need you to need me…"

> "I wish I was an Oscar Meyer Wiener…"

> "Send in the clowns…"

> "I'm climbing the stairway to heaven…"

Answer before thinking.

Let out a primal scream

Lose your cookies

Announce that you are entering a monastery

37

The Aftermath

Don't fool yourself into believing that you're finished once you successfully defend and, if necessary, make the revisions required by your committee. It would be wise to save a good amount of energy for what can be one of the most trying experiences of the doctoral program, one even more difficult than the dissertation itself. I am referring to getting your dissertation bound of course.

Your school wants solid proof that it has just minted a Ph.D. You will likely have to prepare at least two copies of your bound dissertation, one for the library and one for the school archives. This does not mean simply slapping vinyl-covered cardboard on pages of text. It's not that simple. You must follow the rules and procedures. There will likely be a lengthy document that tells you just how wide the margins must be, the size and form of the fonts, how much space between lines, where footnotes go, what they look like, the form of the acknowledgments, and the type of paper you can use (expensive).

Finally, after days, weeks, or months of formatting, printing, copying, and adjusting, you'll bring your bound dissertations to a desk tucked far back in one of the library's alcoves or to some office deep inside the school's tangled bureaucracy. There, you will offer up your monumental work, the dissertation that took up some of the best years of your life. You will expect the librarian or clerk to view your submission with awe, to view you with admiration, and to validate the pride that is bursting forth from the very core of your being. And then, seeing that longing expression on your face, he says "$50 for processing please." "No," you scream. "Do you not realize the magnitude of my accomplishment? Do you have any idea what it took for me to get to this point? I'm a doctor buddy. Have you no sense of decency?" Slowly, his eyes rise to meet yours. You sense victory. You've brought him to his knees with your intellectual mastery, with the power of your story. His lips part and he says "will you be paying with a personal check or a credit card?"

" YOUR DISSERTATION? FINE. IT WILL BE CATALOGUED UNDER 'WHO CARES?' "

38

Free at Last

You're a doctor. You've paid your dues. Now it's out into the "real world." Finishing your dissertation is a little like surfacing after a long, underwater scuba-dive. If you come out too fast, you're likely to get the bends. Slowly ease your way back into society. Take time to reconnect with the things you used to take for granted, like taking a long walk through the woods, hanging out with friends, or having a conversation that doesn't include the word dissertation. Then, after you've had four or five days of this blissful self-indulgence, GET BACK TO WORK! You've got loans to pay off, papers to publish in peer-reviewed journals, tenure-track teaching positions to win, and high-paying consulting jobs to secure. No use savoring the moment. You've got to go, go, go, go.

Actually, people's reactions to becoming a Ph.D. are as varied as the dissertation topics they pursue. Some feel a great sense of loss. Through years of intense work they came to define their world by their research. It created a framework for being, and once it's gone it's like losing the companionship of an old friend or a comforting habit. Others feel like impostors. A Ph.D., rightly or wrongly, anoints you with intellectual credibility. Unfortunately, some Ph.D. programs do such a good job of breaking you down and ruining your self-esteem that their graduates are less confident than when they entered the program. Without a supportive environment and concerned mentors, the dissertation process can leave deep scars on those who battle through until the end, which may not heal for years, if ever. Still others are exhilarated upon completion. Their years as a doctoral student were an intellectual feast that they greedily consumed. With those three letters at the end of their name they are sure of their abilities and eager to take up new challenges.

I finished my defense at 3 in the afternoon on a soggy winter's day. I was both elated and dazed. Walking through the halls of my school was like a dream. It dawned on me that the entire campus, all of the buildings, the paths, the lawns, and the people had suddenly become part of my past. I was moving on to a new phase of my life. I started calling everyone who had been so important to me during these years to tell them the news and thank them for being there. My parents were ecstatic, as were my in-laws. Friends who had seen me through my most difficult times offered congratulations. But the one person who meant the most to me, my wife, would have to wait. She had arranged to take me to dinner that night, regardless of the outcome. I decided not to call her at work. I wanted to see her reaction.

At around 7 p.m. she strode toward me with a wary expression on her face. As she reached out to hug me, I told her I had passed. She hung on tight as I lifted her off the ground and let out a yell. Then I had the best meal of my life and I don't even remember what I ate.

39

Just the Beginning

A Ph.D. is a beginning, not an end. It provides you with the tools to pursue your goals as a researcher, academic, consultant, or whatever. If your program is a good one you'll never look at the world in the same way. It may be subtle or obvious, but from now on you'll take the skills you've acquired and apply them throughout your life. You'll attack problems and questions with a deeper desire to understand how things got to be the way they are and how they might be changed or improved. The desire to ask "why" and to find out the relationship between cause and effect will be strong. You'll have to face up to it sooner or later; you've become a real nerd.

Don't let your ego get too big. Your degree doesn't make you better than anyone else. And it doesn't make you infallible. You will continue to make mistakes. The first mistake might be the dissertation itself, as was the case for a friend of mine. His research was extremely technical, involving physics and chemistry. Shortly after receiving his degree, he published his findings in a prestigious journal. A couple of months after it appeared he realized that one of the fundamental assumptions in his analysis was wrong. This meant that his findings were fallacious, or at least not supported by the data. And now his mistake was immortalized in print. To his credit, my friend did not bemoan his misfortune. He chalked it up to experience, got a few laughs out of it, and went on to the next challenge.

So, congratulations, you made it. Now, get over yourself.

About the Author

Eric Jay Dolin, Ph.D., has published more than sixty articles and seven books, including the *Smithsonian Book of National Wildlife Refuges*, *Snakehead: A Fish Out of Water*, and *Political Waters*. Educated at Brown University, the Yale School of Forestry and Environmental Studies, and the Massachusetts Institute of Technology, his work experience includes being a program manager at the U.S. Environmental Protection Agency, a Knauss Sea Grant Fellow at the U.S. National Oceanic and Atmospheric Administration (NOAA), an environmental consultant, a Pew Research Fellow at Harvard Law School, and an American Association for the Advancement of Science writing fellow at *Business Week*. He currently works as a fisheries policy analyst at NOAA's National Marine Fisheries Service, while living in Marblehead, Massachusetts, with his wife and family.

About the Cartoonist

Dave Carpenter has been a full time cartoonist since 1981. His cartoons have appeared in a number of publications, including the *Harvard Business Review*, *Barron's*, *The Wall Street Journal*, *Reader's Digest*, *Good Housekeeping*, *Better Homes & Gardens*, *The Saturday Evening Post*, as well as in a number of the *Chicken Soup for the Soul* books. Dave has also illustrated comic strips, posters, greeting cards, and magazine articles and covers. He is a member of the National Cartoonist Society and Cartoonist Association. He can be reached at davecarp@ncn.net, and his website is www.carptoons.com.

978-0-595-35030-8
0-595-35030-5

Made in the USA
Middletown, DE
27 March 2025